THE
PRACTICAL
PSYCHIC

Hi Rick,
    Thanks for everything.

        John

THE
PRACTICAL
PSYCHIC

**John Friedlander
and Cynthia Pearson**

SAMUEL WEISER, INC.
York Beach, Maine

First published in 1991 by
Samuel Weiser, Inc.
Box 612
York Beach, Maine 03910

Library of Congress Cataloging-in-Publication Data

Friedlander, John.
    The practical psychic / John Friedlander and Cynthia
Pearson.
      p. cm.
    1. Psychic ability. 2. Parapsychology. I. Pearson,
Cynthia. II. Title.
  BF1040.F75 1991
  133.8—dc20   90-23601
                                            CIP

ISBN 0-87728-728-7
BJ

Cover art is a painting entitled "The Guide,"
© 1991 Clayton Anderson. Used by kind permission of
the artist.

Typeset in 11 point Palatino.

Printed in the United States of America

TABLE OF CONTENTS

For the professors in our lives

ACKNOWLEDGMENTS

We are very grateful to the people who have helped us bring this book into existence. We'd like to thank our agent, Tom Roberts, for helping us know we had found just the right publisher. We want to thank John's students, from whom he learned so much, and all the people who read and reread our many drafts and made so many useful suggestions. This is a long list and includes: Robi Bendorf, Nore DiNardo, Barbara Dinsmore, Linda Diane Feldt, Cora Fetchko, Emil Friedlander, Teresa Friedlander, Judy Irvin Hall, Anne Kuhn, Evelyn Pearson, Mary Stoyer, Peggy Stubbs, Sam Turich and Helen Vantine.

No one was more exacting and more helpful in early editing than Pamela Moss. Tom Turich was generous with his time and computer expertise. We thank Courtney Turich for serving as occasional handmaiden, and the folks at *Sign of Aquarius* bookstore for their occasional handholding. We felt blessed to have Dianne Kelleher's psychic guidance and spiritual companionship.

We want to express our appreciation to all the knowledgeable people at Weiser. Their love for the subject matter is genuine and gratifying.

Finally, no book would have been possible if it weren't for the numerous teachers that John has been privileged to study with. Especially important to this book have been Lewis Bostwick, Jane Roberts, and Seth.

INTRODUCTION

Welcome to the world of the practical psychic. This useful, pleasant, approach to psychic development is based upon the unique background of John Friedlander.

John studied with the most accomplished psychics of our time and then learned how to successfully apply esoteric principles in the workaday world. The most important figure in John's psychic development was Jane Roberts and her trance personality, Seth. John's education also includes personal study with Lewis Bostwick, founder of the Berkeley Psychic Institute; travel in India to study meditation; a degree from Harvard Law School; and fifteen years of practicing law.

From this perspective, John developed a way of using psychic techniques in practical reality that he has been teaching for years. His system brings concepts that have been considered the province of great mystics into the ordinary dimensions of human life. The system marries the unlimited and the limited, and like marriages in general, offers a forum in which love can be explored and fulfilled.

The Practical Psychic may sound like a contradiction, but that's precisely the point. In order to become truly competent psychically, you must be competent in everyday life, and vice versa. However, competence should not be considered a promise of perfection or transcendence.

John likes to illustrate this distinction with the story about his brother Charlie, who at age 5 ran for president of his kindergarten. Charlie's opponent promised his classmates that everyone who voted for him would get a pony. Charlie countered with a promise that everyone who voted for him would get a swimming pool in their backyard. We do not promise that you can wish things into being, "Abracadabra." Being a practical psychic is an encounter with the joys and frustrations of physical life.

In this book, you will learn techniques that help you enlist the enormous resources of your psychic ability. Beyond techniques, we have attempted to give you a picture, a story, a feeling of how the psychic life actually works. You will be able to proceed step-by-step as if you were in one of John's classes, with illustrations from his experience as a teacher, psychic and lawyer. In the second half of the book, you will learn techniques for making long-term and sweeping changes in your life. But throughout the book, our theme remains the same—that you, standing here in the bookstore scanning this page, may not get a pony or a swimming pool in your backyard, but we can guarantee that you have a profound spiritual mission. It is to live your life, ordinary and sublime.

That life, ordinary and sublime, is the purpose of this book.

1 Becoming a Practical Psychic

HUMAN BEINGS HAVE always longed for more power over their lives. The allure of becoming psychic is a reflection of this wish—one that has persisted through centuries and across cultures. It is the premise of this book that mankind's wish has already been granted.

At the end of *The Wizard of Oz,* Dorothy learns that she has had the power to return home all along, but she didn't know it. When she learns the technique of clicking her heels together, she's immediately on her way.

We provide you with techniques to get you where you want to go, too. The techniques won't be much harder than clicking your heels together. You needn't possess special talents or abilities; you needn't be clairvoyant or telepathic or precognitive. To become a practical psychic, you can be as ordinary as a Kansas farm girl. Everyone reading this book can use the techniques successfully.

THE PRACTICAL PSYCHIC

The reason you can become a practical psychic is because you create your own reality. Reality creation occurs in an interaction with a greater dimension, which may be called God, or All That Is. Actually, it occurs in a discrete portion of All That Is which has been called the higher self, the oversoul, the ground of your being, the entity, the God of your heart, and other names. We will use the term "deep self."

The deep self seems different from what you ordinarily think of as yourself, and yet your consciousness and reality rise out of it, much as a plant rises out of the earth. At times, you can even experience the entirety of the deep self in a union that many religious mystics have described as a union with God.

Your deep self creates your reality, but does so in a way that reflects your ordinary consciousness. Since the creation of your reality relies upon the interaction of your deep self with your ordinary consciousness, the most effective way to improve your reality is to improve the quality of that interaction.

You, the ordinary you, are already involved in that interaction without being aware of it.

The Conventional Psychic Vs. the Practical Psychic

Usually the term "psychic" refers to someone who has developed paranormal abilities and can consciously make use of them. We call this being a conventional psychic, and John has been one for most of his adult life. His experiences led him to recognize that abilities such as telepathy and clairvoyance were simply efficient techniques for acquiring information. What is far more important, he discovered, is improving the instructions you send to the deep self. This is relatively easy to do because the primary tools for improving those instructions can be accessed with your conscious mind.

Becoming a practical psychic means developing the ability to work consciously and deliberately with the deep self. This book teaches techniques to do that. It provides common sense ways of organizing those techniques within the experience of your everyday life. Conventional psychic talents and abilities are helpful but not required. In fact, people with no psychic gifts sometimes succeed where some conventional psychics fail.

THE ONE AND ONLY YOU

The relationship between you and your deep self is and will be absolutely unique. The instructions and guidance offered here are not like a recipe with which, upon following each direction precisely, you produce exactly the same dish that the author has concocted. On the contrary, the whole point of becoming a practical psychic is to skillfully cook up your own reality.

William Blake said, "I must create a system, or be enslav'd by another man's."[1] The most important premise of the practical psychic is that each reader and student is embarked on his or her own journey of the soul. Therefore, everything else—practices, exercises, programs, systems—must be in service to each individual path. As you read and begin using the exercises here, understand that they are meant to guide you into your own unique experience.

THE THREE STEPS OF THE PRACTICAL PSYCHIC

According to a great musician, "First you learn how to play notes, then you learn how to play sounds, and then you learn how to play jazz." There is a similar progression for the practical psychic. The exercises you will learn in this book are meant to make it simple for you to work with the deep self. These are the notes you learn to play.

---

[1] William Blake, *The Portable Blake* (New York: Viking Press, 1946), p. 460.

Built into the exercises is the intention that each of you be able to make them work in your personal life. In order to avoid creating an opposition between the material and the spiritual, we encourage you to look to your own life and values to seek and judge what is working for you. This integration and application of psychic techniques into your own life are the sounds you will learn.

Finally, there are deeper lessons built into this approach. It is designed to enhance your engagement—your love, courage and sense of play—in your life. The engagement required to put the pieces together brings you into touch with a vibrant, creative spirituality that flows naturally, like your own spontaneous jazz.

2 Balance and Harmony

THE FOUNDATION OF THE practical psychic approach is understanding the importance of balance and harmony. You may recall Walt Disney's cartoon version of *The Sorcerer's Apprentice*. In it, Mickey Mouse plays the title character, a novice who decides to expropriate some of his master's supernatural powers to perform his janitorial duties. Figuring that what worked for the sorcerer should work just as well for him, poor Mickey suffers disastrous results.

The sorcerer's apprentice made the mistake of thinking that mere power could solve his problems. He did not understand that the sorcerer had spent the time needed to learn not only the power of magic, but the balance and harmony necessary to use it. The apprentice used magic as if it were a mechanical operation instead of a mystical approach to living. In order for techniques to be effective, they need to be meaningfully integrated into your life.

THE MAGIC OF RECONCILING OPPOSITES

Many of us study yoga when we first become interested in consciousness and spirituality. The first thing you learn in yoga is that every time you bend or stretch in one direction, you must bend or stretch in the other.

A practical psychic integrates opposites in this fashion. For example, when you understand that you create your own reality, you might think you can have anything. In a sense, you can, and it's very important to understand the mind-boggling levels of freedom you do have. Your effectiveness as a practical psychic will be severely limited if you are not able to invoke this enormous freedom.

Yet you have to balance this power with a willingness to appreciate whatever manages to happen. The purpose of your experience is to have it. You must be open and receptive to life on its own terms. Appreciate the experience you have, and accept the practical limits on your ability to control life, even as you understand the possibility at every point to change your life for the better. It is precisely such an ability to dynamically balance opposites like these that leads to becoming a practical psychic.

The balance of opposites is not a static one, but a mobile and flexible balance responsive to changing situations. If you are sailing on the ocean and you want to make good time, you will want to raise every sail. If, however, you are caught in a terrible squall, your best strategy will be to lower your sails and ride out the storm. It is the ability to live your life in an everchanging harmony and balance that fills your reality with magic, meaning and grace.

A Psychic Exercise

There are several purposes served in the following exercise, each having to do with enlarging your sense of the possibilities available to you. It has been said that we are "binary thinkers." We tend to break things down into pairs of opposites and seek to understand our world in terms of polarities. Whether the dualities are good vs. evil, war and peace, heaven or hell, the effect is the same—we end up limited to "either/or" conclusions.

Let's take an example near and dear to our hearts. This book is called *The Practical Psychic*. Obviously, we think that being practical is really important, but if we allowed practicality to become an overriding virtue, we would limit ourselves. Someone obsessed with practicality might lose the ability to be playful or adventurous. At times, being downright silly is not only fun, it is creative!

Whenever you allow any virtue to become obsessively important, that very virtue begins to crowd out the free play and exploration of your consciousness. By cultivating a recognition that every virtue has seeming opposites that can also be virtues, you will be moving a long way toward one of the most important qualities of being a practical psychic—nonjudgmentalness. The development of non-judgmentalness really frees up your power to be loving, and to flow.

Exercise 1
Opposing Virtues

Think of virtues that are of primary importance to you, virtues that seem essential. Then think of some opposites that are favorable, and some synonyms that are unfavorable. Note that the so-called opposites are not really exclusive of one another. You can be both adventurous and practical, for example. However, too great a concern with any one virtue can lead you to ignore other balancing virtues.

The Central Challenge

The central challenge is to apply any psychic approach in balance and harmony. Learning magical techniques is not hard, but simply learning the techniques is not the main objective of the practical psychic. Learning to apply them with grace and common sense is.

Every chapter in this book deals directly or indirectly with balance and harmony. You will be using the power of the deep self, but you must balance and harmonize that power with strong, coordinated conscious efforts, taking practical, worldly steps to reach your goals. You will be learning how to balance making things happen with allowing and trusting them to happen. You will learn balance for—among other things—choice and cooperation, striving and surrendering, taking chances and staying safe.

We like to tell students about John's experience growing up in Georgia. He was a high school football player, a strapping young man, when he went to work one summer as a ditch digger and general laborer. On the job was a pot-bellied old man who astounded John by digging three times faster than he could. The old man couldn't have had John's strength or stamina, but he did have experience. His integrated know-how was in every way superior to John's raw power. The old man knew when and how to conserve his power; he knew when and how to make subtle adjustments. This is an example of the kind of practical balance and harmony we want to establish.

The first harmony you need to develop is that of the deep self and the conscious self.

3 Balancing the Deep Self with the Conscious Self

MANY SPIRITUAL SEEKERS are convinced that they are here on earth to rise above their "low" vibrations, or follow the commands of "higher consciousness," as if the very purpose of being human were to rise above their humanness. This is the "Life is a Trick Question" approach. It assumes that life experience is something to escape from. It also assumes that life is some sort of cosmic prank. Such an approach is both negative and misleading, for it neglects the special place in creation occupied by each of its parts, one of which is you.

Jesus said that not even one sparrow falls without God's attention and caring. A sparrow is important not because it will one day evolve into a superior being, but because it is unique and wonderful, in and of itself. At least as much is true of a human being. You may evolve through many incarnations, but your life also has importance and meaning right now. It had importance and meaning yesterday, and it will again tomorrow, no matter how desolate the circumstances in which you may find yourself.

Now the practical significance of the "non-trickiness" of your life is enormous, though not immediately obvious. It means that you, at each moment, have a simple, accessible tool to make your life more meaningful and pleasant. That tool is, believe it or not, your conscious mind.

:

To fully appreciate the power of your conscious mind, you should understand that your deep self's separate purposes are best served by its manifesting a personal reality for you that reflects your conscious self with all its strengths, conflicts and absurdities.

THE DEEP SELF

Following the lead of Jane Roberts, we call the entirety of creation and God and whatever, "All That Is." The portion of All That Is that creates your daily world we call the deep self. Like the producer of a movie, your deep self assembles all the actors and raw materials you need to bring about the events in your life. It works just outside the boundaries of space and time, placing events into the fabric of your days seamlessly, so that in space and time, you are the creator of your experience according to the laws and limitations of our world.

Your deep self follows a self-imposed law. The events it drops into your life follow the directions of your conscious self. Unfortunately, one is not usually aware of the magical relationship between the conscious mind and the deep self, and often unaware of the difficulties caused by hidden or transparent beliefs. Those beliefs can lead to your giving poor directions to the deep self. Learning to be a practical psychic means learning how to give good directions to your deep self.

THE DEEP SELF IS
CONSCIOUS AND LIVELY

Because of our society's programming about human psychology, you might be inclined to think of the deep self as unconscious. Actually, at its deepest portions, the deep self becomes like God, with a sharper, clearer, more complete consciousness than we ever achieve in our separated selves. It is the wellspring that all mystics seek to join. At less deep levels the deep self can be viewed as personal guides, masters, angels or whatever, very conscious.

Just as All That Is breaks itself up into portions to create you, the other people in the world, and the world itself; so it breaks itself up at other dimensions to create autonomous personalities with different or even superhuman powers. These guides and "masters" are no more and no less separated from All That Is than you are. They have their own purposes, which may be incomprehensible at times. Still, you can generally understand what your deep self wants in relation to you.

THE DEEP SELF IS UNIFIED WITH YOU

Mystics throughout the ages have taught that you have inner connections with everything that exists—physical or non-physical—and with every event that happens to you. This fundamental union extends to the deep self that forms your human reality; that deep self is you. This is why we call it the deep self.

Just as you are unified with All That Is—including the deep self—so from the perspective of the deep self, it is unified with you. Furthermore, just as you have much to gain from it, it profits from relating to you.

THE DEEP SELF USES YOUR EXPERIENCE

There is a mostly hidden mystical tradition that people's lives, emotions, thoughts and deeds provide "food" for God. You might say you are "God's Little Acre." The particular portion of God that you provide for is your deep self.

This tradition can seem to reduce humankind to a lowly function, but it is really an attempt to describe the mystical union of humans and All That Is. You, along with other people and things, are inside of God in general and inside various deep selves in particular. Your deep self is nourished by the crops of your experiences. It is important to cultivate your own choices. If you don't, your deep self goes hungry.

The Deep Self's Purpose Requires Your Independence

When you have a child, you expect that this child will grow to be a healthy adult. But if you were to say about childhood, as some long-faced New Agers say about life, that the purpose of childhood is adulthood, and that childhood is a trap to be escaped from by concentrating on maturity, both you and your child would miss the joy of experiencing childhood. Your children's experiences are their own, yet you may derive joy and insight from their presence and example. Your deep self is like an infinitely loving and wise parent, only in this case you continue to reside inside the deep self's larger being.

A child's success depends on the child's development of a strong, independent identity. Wise and loving parents encourage that development, even as they feel the child is a fulfillment of their own purposes. Similarly, your deep self—for purposes of its own explorations—gives birth to you, fully understanding that you must develop your independence.

A toddler cannot understand the amused joy of a grandparent who watches as the child runs with innocent energy and abandon. You may not understand the joy that your deep self takes in your experiences either, but it is there. Furthermore, a grandparent could never experience a grandchild's vitality if the child spent his or her youth obsessed with escaping from childhood. Just as it would defeat the delight of the grandparent to suppress the child's exuberance, so would it defeat the purpose of the deep self to suppress your self-discovery.

THE DEEP SELF DOES NOT LIMIT YOUR CHOICES

Sometimes parents offer a child freedom to make choices with the proviso that the choices had better be the right ones! The deep self has no such agenda. There are almost always numerous choices fully satisfactory to the deep self. This is one of the hardest points to realize because it goes against your preconceptions. It doesn't usually matter to your deep self what job you choose or what other major decisions you make. What is important is how a decision fits into a meaningful life—and almost any considered, vibrant choice will do. You are the one who sets the priorities, such as how important making considerably more money is to you, or whether you truly want to be married. While the deep self can provide enormous help in evaluating the wisdom of various choices, you set the priorities which lead to your deep self's fulfillment.

It is important to appreciate the real value of your experiences. People do change and develop through countless experiences, and this growth is half of the balance we have been stressing. It is true that all people will evolve into higher planes, but saying that growth is the sole purpose of life wrenches evolution from the very "flow" that higher planes require. The other half of the balance is the value of the experience itself. This other half—experience, for its own sake—is what you must pay attention to. Experience itself, whatever your choices are, is what the deep self supports and facilitates.

The reality created by the deep self is a representation in space and time of your conscious self with all its conflicts, strengths and absurdities. Your deep self is giving you a drama that fully expresses who you are at the moment. There will be parts you love and parts you want to change. As you experience this drama that is you, you change and grow, and so the deep self creates new dramas, new realities, day by day. In this way, you emotionally experience the implications of those conflicts, strengths and absurdities of your conscious mind. In ways incomprehensible to humankind, your deep self uses your emotional experiences for its own loving purposes.

COMMUNICATING WITH THE DEEP SELF

In the early days of attempting to create his own reality, John felt very macho about the whole thing. He wanted to force reality into a mold of his choosing. In fact, he thought he had a spiritual obligation to evolve into a person who could make everything happen just the way he wanted it to happen.

Now he views it more as an interactive undertaking, like horseback riding. His conscious mind rides the deep self like a rider on a horse. The major difference is that the horse, the deep self, is more conscious than he is—and yet, the deep self carries him wherever he directs it.

The techniques in this book are designed to lead you into a warm and productive relationship with your deep self. There is an inexhaustible energy available to you. Now you are learning how to use it.

4 The Practical Fantasizer

ONE OF THE MOST powerful tools of the practical psychic is the imagination. "Practical fantasizing" is the directed and focused use of the imagination, and there are a number of psychic exercises in this book based on it.

The next exercise uses the metaphor of the rider and horse to enhance your understanding of the co-equal nature of the conscious self and the deep self. It has two objectives. The first is to help you understand and trust the horse, the deep self; and the second is to help you accept the role of your conscious mind as the rider, the one with responsibility for deciding the direction in which you travel.

Now this exercise is not focused on any particular physical goal. It will increase your harmony and balance, which in turn will increase the level of cooperation and communication between your conscious self and the deep self.

To get underway, sit in a comfortable chair, take a few deep breaths, relax and give yourself over to a state of deliberate daydreaming. Two to five minutes is about right for any one exercise.

EXERCISE 2
PSYCHIC HORSEBACK RIDING

To begin, in your mind's eye mount your horse and settle comfortably into the saddle. Survey the scene from the

rider's perspective and call up the scent of horseflesh. As
your horse begins a slow walk, feel it move beneath you.
Hear the leather creak and the hoofs gently plodding.
Holding the reins and gripping with your knees, note the
communication between you and the animal. You are co-
equal. Understand that the deep self carries you at your
directions.

The exercise you have just completed is the basis for a
series of fantasies. This is a good place to discuss some
basics.

FANTASIZING 101

1) Practical fantasizing is both a psychic and a physical operation. As you practice it, you are changing your aura,
your brain and your body. We call this your psychic biology. Changing your psychic biology means changing your
psychic atmosphere, and thus also your reality.

2) Don't sweat it. However you fantasize is okay. You may
want to sit in a comfortable chair or you may prefer to lie
down (although you might defeat your purpose by falling
asleep). Some people may vividly experience the feel,
smell and sight of a horse. However, it is also sufficient to
simply think through the idea. There are no limits to, or
laws governing, styles of fantasizing. You can hold a static
image, or imagine events unfolding in time. Do it the way
you enjoy it.

3) Expect changes to take time. Many people will experience alterations almost immediately, but some will take a
couple of months. Eventually, you will find that beneficial
changes can result from even very small alterations.

4) The central aim of practical fantasizing is to make life
better by improving the cooperation between the con-

scious mind and the deep self. However, a common by-product is that many will find they are developing as conventional psychics. This can be both fun and useful.

5) There are several styles of fantasizing, based on the different sensory modes—seeing, hearing, touching, tasting, and smelling. Some of them will be naturally more enjoyable and useful to you than others. However, it's a good idea to try them all.

6) Just as you will find you have favorite styles of fantasizing, you will also find that some of the exercises are more useful for you than others. By all means, concentrate on the exercises that are most useful for you, but do give each one a try for at least three days.

To get the most out of your fantasizing, find a comfortable spot where you won't be disturbed. Let other members of the household know that this is your time for yourself. Turn off the phone and any other distractions in your immediate vicinity. Sit in a comfortable chair. Relax with a few deep breaths and begin the exercise you've chosen. Do the exercise in a playful, unhurried way. It helps to smile to yourself from time to time. Allow the exercise to unfold in your mind.

Whichever exercise you do, spend two to five minutes on it from one to four times a day. On any given day, limit yourself to only one or two different exercises, because this gives your body and mind time to derive maximum benefits. However, serial exercises, such as the horse and rider exercises given throughout this chapter, can be joined together when you have become an experienced fantasizer.

Finally, even though the exercises could be called visualizations, we use the term "fantasies" because their primary objective is the fun of doing them. We also want to stress that imagination is your most important psychic tool. With practice, you will become so skillful at using your imagination that you will eventually cease to wonder what is "just your imagination" and what is your psychic ability.

THREE ASPECTS OF FANTASIZING

In the psychic horseback riding exercise, we asked you to see, hear and feel elements of the fantasy in your imagination. Using a variety of sensory modes will help you to get more out of all the fantasies you'll be given in this book. Here is a description of the three main styles of sensory fantasizing, with suggestions for using each of them:

♦ To fantasize VISUALLY, you summon up images in your mind's eye. (The easiest example for most people is a sexual fantasy.) One visual technique is to imagine that you see a photograph. In your mind's eye, you may look at it closely, or keep it at a distance. You can make the image fuzzy or clear, static or moving. You can take features out or add things that weren't there to begin with. You can burn, dissolve or otherwise destroy a picture; you can also enlarge, mount or frame it. As the saying goes, "Seeing is believing."

♦ Fantasizing AURALLY can entail listening to the voice of another, or to your own voice, out loud or in your mind. You may simply tell a story, recounting to yourself, or to a listener, the events of your fantasy. You can engage in a dialogue with others, verbalizing the role of each party. Also, verbalization doesn't have to be oral. Writing a fantasy uses different portions of the brain, and that is an advantage that often outweighs the possible loss of spontaneity. In all cases, you can edit features in or out, or completely change the account.

♦ PHYSICAL fantasizing is non-verbal. With it, you focus on tactile sensations such as warmth, or roughness. For example, if someone wishes to overcome a fear of flying, he or she could use the sensory technique to imagine a parallel situation that is pleasurable, such as riding in a sporty convertible on a beautiful day. Calling up the physical delights of the drive, the traveler can then imaginatively transfer those sensations to an airplane ride. The point is to bring in some positive sensations and feelings while letting the negative ones diminish.

Most people naturally gravitate to one of these three styles. Smell and taste can also be used, but usually not as primary sensory styles. When you are first learning an exercise, concentrate on the style that comes most easily. Most exercises will be improved, however, if you enhance them with as many different types of sensory details as you can. Add imaginative elements from the other senses as you become more familiar with each exercise. Finally, if you're having trouble engaging any mode, you can summon the senses by getting up and acting out an imaginary script you make up as you go along like a child at play.

CHECK YOUR FEELINGS

One of the most important goals of practical fantasizing is to get in touch with your feelings around the exercise. For example, suppose you start on the horse and rider exercise and find that you fear the horse. If that is the case, try another animal—an ox, a porpoise, or an eagle perhaps, and see if that works. If it doesn't, then you probably fear some aspect of the deep self. Ask yourself what's wrong. You will usually get a sense of the problem. It could be that you think of the deep self as too powerful, in which case you could make the horse gentler, sweeter. You could give it some sugar, or gain confidence by walking with it on a lead. This is your fantasy, be creative! Now, if your fear persists, good. That's right, good, because as you work day after day on resolving your fear, deep reorganizations will take place in your body and mind. You are changing yourself for the better.

Don't go out looking for fears and hesitations in your fantasy where there are none, but do pay attention to your emotions as they rise. Build on your enjoyable emotions and change your unpleasant ones.

Remember that fantasizing works best in a playful frame of mind. Therefore, as you're beginning, don't feel compelled to choose the most important issues of your life. You can begin with simple, less momentous issues. With the next three exercises, remember to enjoy yourself.

Exercise 3
Horse and Rider Dialogue

In this exercise, you select one issue about which you would like to have a dialogue with your deep self. It may be specific ("How can I ask my boss for a raise?") or general ("How can I be more assertive?"). You may fantasize that your horse talks to you directly; or that it carries you to a person who tells you something; or that it takes you to a picture of information that will help you.

Don't do just anything your horse suggests. Do only what makes sense. On the other hand, don't stop listening to your horse too soon. If it gives you advice that seems inexplicable or even weird, that might be an indication that you don't understand just what issues are involved. Therefore, before you abandon your deep self's advice, engage in conversation with it. Tell it just why its advice seems inappropriate. Ask it if there's some point that you may have overlooked. Cultivate a relationship with your deep self that encourages dialogue, exploration and communion.

EXERCISE 4
HORSE AND RIDER MERGER

Shift your focus back and forth from the horse to the rider. Alternately imagine yourself as the horse and the rider. This paradoxical exercise tends to develop the understanding that, "There are no boundaries to the self."[1] This exercise has the potential to lead you directly to a transcendent mystical experience, but in any case it will increase your sense of connectedness with the deep self.

EXERCISE 5
HORSE AND RIDER MANIFESTATION

Picture an event you want to have occur and then have your horse take you to it. You may even have your horse fly you there, if you are then careful to bring your image down to earth afterward. (You don't want to leave it in the clouds, where it can't manifest.) Once you have arrived, use your imagination to enter into the event. Practice all sensory styles to see, hear and feel that event. This exercise fully communicates your desires to the deep self, while allowing your personality to make the adjustments which permit the event to happen.

COMMON EXPERIENCES WITH
HORSE AND RIDER EXERCISES

There are two common difficulties that students have with these exercises. First, some students approach the exercise

---

[1]Seth frequently reminded us of this throughout our classes as well as his books.

by trying to figure out where the horse wants to go. While being attentive to the horse/deep self is important, you need to acknowledge your job as the rider. You and the deep self are co-equal. So have the horse take you where you want to go. Of course, if your horse balks, your deep self may be trying to give you good information. Ask yourself why it is balking. Ask your horse where it wants to go and why and how your route may be inappropriate. Take a few days or weeks to explore the hesitations if you need to. Your deep self may have wonderful information for you, but you decide. Try different paths to get where you want to go. As long as you are open and playful, you will get the insight you need sooner or later.

Secondly, sometimes students find themselves falling off their horses. Remember, you can use your difficulties to learn what your resistances are. Usually people who fall off their horses are expressing resistance to the idea of being carried and helped by the horse, feeling they must "gut out" a challenge on their own. In the horse and rider exercises, it is important to gain a sense of being carried and supported. This will open the channels to the help and support available from the deep self without any other exercises. You may not be consciously aware of the increased help and support all the time, but it will be there.

Finally, with these and all other exercises, it may take practice before you can proceed comfortably. The old saying about getting back on the horse is as true in fantasy as reality, and holds for any obstacles encountered in fantasizing. Take your time and understand that you are transforming your aura, body and brain.

5 Significance of Feeling Tones

DON'T BE A SCROOGE;
He's a real Casanova;
She's such a Pollyanna.

From such descriptions, you readily understand that the party in question is mean spirited, aggressively amorous, or sickeningly optimistic. You may also observe among friends and relatives those perpetually plagued by misfortune, and those who always seem to luck out—those who see life as an entertaining adventure and others who cower at the approach of the paperboy. Some people thrive on crisis; others wilt under pressure. These are all examples of our perceptions of the feeling tones of others.[1]

We all evaluate feeling tones constantly. Any painting by Renoir evokes a very different tone than one by Picasso. A Christmas carol sung by a child will affect us very differently than the same one sung by an adult professional. Enduringly popular entertainers, such as Bob Hope or George Burns, exude a sense of amused wisdom and joy in life, and these feeling tones affect their audiences at least as much as any of their jokes.

Your feeling tones influence both inner and outer levels of your experience. Think, for example, of the psychic

---

[1]Seth described feeling tones as "emotional attitudes toward yourself and life in general, and these generally govern the large areas of experience." Jane Roberts, *The Nature of Personal Reality* (New York: Prentice Hall, 1974), p. 13.

magnetism of someone who has fallen in love. Not only does he or she experience an inward elation; the smitten individual also discovers that the external world has improved markedly. As the saying goes, "everybody loves a lover," because someone in love exudes happiness and well-being.

Your overall feeling tones don't change with your daily moods. They're more constant and embedded in your psychic biology. However, there are exercises to change them. In the following exercises, you will be asked to both evaluate and then alter your own feeling tones.

Exercise 6
The House Fantasy

Picture a house in your mind's eye. Have the intention that this house will symbolically represent you, that it will have your "energy." Just have the intention, and the energy will take care of itself. It can be any sort of house you wish. Go inside and enter one of the rooms. Look around this room. What are the furnishings like? What colors are in it? Is there anything on the walls? Is it comfortable? Walk around and experience the room in as much detail as you can.

For the second part of the exercise, think of what changes you might like to make in that room. Would you like it to serve a different function—be a library instead of a dining room? What furnishings would you prefer? What colors? Is there in your memory a room or style of decor you would like to incorporate? Illustrations from a book, scenes from a movie, photographs from magazines can all be called upon to prime your imagination. The point is to re-do the room so that it pleases you. Don't push yourself on this one. You can take your time and change the room day by day as you feel comfortable with the changes.

Now if your easiest mode of fantasizing is aural or tactile, then you will want to transform this and other exercises. For example, imagine that you go into a house and hear sounds, perhaps a baby crying or music playing. Then change any sounds you want to change. You might hear the baby breathing contentedly or turn the music into singing.

Exercise 7
To Dream Again

Dreams are valuable resources because in them feeling tones are experienced directly and immediately. In this exercise, you make use of a dream that you would like to change. Often, nightmares are the first examples that come to mind, but the dream you choose needn't be traumatic. It only needs to contain an element that you would like to make different. Remember it in as much detail as possible, writing it down if you haven't already.

In a relaxed state, re-dream your dream in your imagination. Don't go to sleep, just re-experience the feeling as much as possible. When you get to the part you want to change, do so.

For example, suppose you've dreamed of driving, losing control of your car and plunging into a river. You might re-dream this experience so you regain control of the car and maneuver it back onto the road. Or re-dream that as your car plunged toward the river, it was able to fly aloft; or that upon landing in the river, your car turned out to be amphibious and cruised through the water.

There are different ways to proceed with this exercise. You can make a series of changes in one dream, or work changes through several dreams. You can explore several ways to change a single dream item. You can retell yourself your changed dream, much as you might recall an ordinary dream, in order to reinforce the change. Write down the changed dream in your dream notebook, just as if it had been a "real" dream.

This is a potent exercise. It can help you alter your own limitations, your relationships with others, and the distortions of society and culture at large.

Working with feeling tones is like spreading paint with a large roller. You can cover, change and improve large areas. Similarly, improving your feeling tones will result in improvements that spread throughout large portions of your life. For example, becoming more contented and feeling more deserving will make people respond more favorably to you. However, you can't use a roller to paint details. You need a fine brush for that.

The "brush" you use to paint the details of your experience is working with beliefs, a practical psychic tool that is discussed in the next three chapters.

6 The Power of Beliefs in Theory

SETH'S DICTUM, "YOU create your own reality according to your beliefs," is perhaps the central principle of the New Age. No other concept is as useful for remaking lives, adding effectiveness, and enriching meaning.

To use the power of beliefs well requires a deep understanding of what beliefs are. As is often the case with New Age thought, words do not readily express the underlying truths. English has no word for these multidimensional sparks of life we call beliefs. Beliefs are structured by thoughts, but they are more than mere notions. Beliefs are imbued with physical, emotional, intellectual and spiritual potency.

HOW BELIEFS WORK

Your beliefs act as personal boundaries between you and the deep self. They perform a function similar to the one performed by the walls of the cells of your body. The cell wall forms a semipermeable membrane that lets in nutrients from the whole body; it also serves to keep inappropriate substances out. In much the same way, your beliefs form a wall of psychic identity that admits some events from your deep self while preventing others from entering.

The deep self has the ability to manifest any physical experience for you, to give you whatever your heart desires, but it must follow rules. Remember, your experience as an individual with a conscious mind is important to the deep self. The way the deep self manifests experience for you while honoring your autonomy is to follow your beliefs.

Your beliefs form a sphere of availability,[1] setting up what might be called an electromagnetic "self" wall. Just as the whole body cooperates and follows guidelines of the individual cell wall by pushing through just those nutrients the cell wall can and will accept, so the deep self pushes through only what your self wall will permit.

Consequently, if there are events you desire, all you have to do to have them take place is to alter the beliefs in your self wall. Naturally, of course, there's a knack to using the magic of beliefs well and with common sense. For the practical psychic, the first step in developing that ability is understanding what we mean by beliefs.

A Naive Perspective

"That's just a belief!"

John recalls this was everybody's favorite response when he was a member of the Seth classes. In those first attempts to understand Seth's axiom, it was assumed that beliefs were mere intellectual conclusions that insight would enable you to change at will. In those first days, they thought that changing your reality should be as simple as changing your mind. It wasn't, and John's Superman story illustrates why.

When he was about 5 years old, John got the idea that if he went each day to a private spot and wished very hard

---

[1]Ophiel coins the phrase "sphere of availability" in his book *The Art and Practice of Getting Material Things Through Creative Visualization* (York Beach, ME: Samuel Weiser, Inc., 1967), p. 25.

and repetitively, "I wish I were Superman, I wish I were Superman," then he would be able to fly. And so he did go to a private spot and wish very hard that he were Superman. He did this for what seemed to be a very long time—three days—and then proceeded to test out his new ability in a flying leap. He can still hear his breath being knocked out of his lungs as he landed on his stomach.

So sincere and complete was John's belief that he would fly that he hadn't even tried to break his fall with his arms or hands. Today, John uses this experience to describe the subtle and difficult distinctions necessary to understand beliefs.

In any ordinary sense of the word, John *believed* he was going to fly. So obviously if this fundamental principle of the New Age—"You create your own reality according to your beliefs"—is going to have any usefulness, a deeper understanding is necessary.

THE DIFFERENCE BETWEEN A CONCLUSION AND A BELIEF

Beliefs do not operate as simple intellectual packages or conclusions. They differ in two important ways. First, they operate in systems. Secondly, they are not composed merely of intellectual content, but are in a sense living components of your aura, intellect, emotions and physical body.

In our logical, Western tradition, we customarily isolate and take things apart to study them. This is a hard habit to break. The important thing to realize when working with beliefs is that they are not single units, like bricks in a wall. Rather, they influence everything and each other, like the seasonings in a soup. When you taste the soup, you may be able to identify which spices were used, but the overall flavor comes from the blend.

Returning to John's abortive attempt at flight, he had not developed an overall belief that he could fly; rather, he formed a simple conclusion that he would fly. A conclusion is a single, isolated statement, whereas a belief is part of a whole system, a grid of knowledge and understanding.

Even at 5, John's belief system was grounded in his being a human boy rather than a kid from Krypton with powers and abilities far beyond those of mortal men. John knew that humans don't fly, that things fall when you drop them, and numerous other facts of ordinary human existence. This knowledge overwhelmed his simple conclusion that he could fly. In addition to his intellectual knowledge, there were more important reasons John did not fly related to the nature of beliefs.

The belief in gravity was knitted into John's very bones. It is this multidimensional knitting of beliefs into your body, emotions, intellect and aura that we will discuss next. When you understand the interaction of the body, mind and aura, you will understand why, even intellectually, beliefs operate in systems.

Beliefs Are Multidimensional

It's easy to understand that beliefs are multidimensional when you observe a psychic reading. In the next section we're going to describe such a reading, but not because it's necessary to be or consult a conventional psychic. We're doing it because it is the best way to demonstrate the multidimensionality of beliefs, and how they work in systems.

As John was studying to become a conventional psychic, he learned how to give aura readings at Berkeley Psychic Institute under Lewis Bostwick. For over a generation, Bostwick and his students have taught a readily usable system that leads to direct psychic experience.[2] It begins with the understanding that there is such a thing as psychic energy which, like electrical energy, is invisible but potent. You and your body are in, of and comprise a field of psychic energy, taking it in and giving it off much as an organism takes in and gives off air, food and water. You can visualize this energy as a radiant cloud surrounding you, much as Kirlian photographs show a field of light surrounding their subjects. This field is commonly referred to as the aura.

The aura is composed of a number of layers surrounding the body, like concentric shells of energy. Perhaps the simplest way to visualize these layers is to think of nesting dolls, identical figures that fit inside one another. However, you cannot take yourself apart. You and your aura are many layers altogether. Learning to perceive the aura and its layers is part of learning to give psychic readings.

Psychic energy is dynamic, and the aura is constantly changing and active, just as your body is constantly operating. One feature that is especially useful to the psychic reader is an impression of a past event left in the aura, called a "picture." It is like a freeze frame, but instead of frozen motion, a psychic picture is frozen energy. Pictures may appear in any one of the aura's layers. Depending upon the subject's feelings about his or her experiences, pictures carry an emotional "charge" which causes them to collect with other similar pictures. In addition, pictures tend to reveal themselves in specific portions of the body which have a functional purpose correspondent with their emotional charge. For instance, psychically the neck relates to communication with others. Pictures of events and

---

[2]Although Bostwick himself has stated that he never will put his system down in writing, believing in the primary importance of firsthand teaching and experience, several of his students have written helpful guides; see the Recommended Reading section.

ideas that indicate, for example, "I can't say what I really feel" will tend to congregate around the subject's neck.[3]

So when looking at an individual's aura, a psychic reader sees a multidimensional energy system composed of pictures which radiate, the subject's emotions and thoughts about the pictured events; and the portion of the body connected with those pictures. Together, those multidimensional pictures manifest beliefs.

SEEING HOW BELIEFS OPERATE
AN AURA READING

The following account illustrates how deeply and thoroughly beliefs are held, quite literally, within our bodies and minds. It is based on a reading which John performed for Ellen, a client concerned with resuming the writing career she'd deferred while raising a family. In this instance, the purpose of the reading was to "eliminate the negative." It concentrated on those belief pictures that could detract from Ellen's success.[4]

As soon as the reading began, John observed a picture near Ellen's solar plexus, an area associated with ambition. "It looks like your mother told you that you weren't good enough, that you didn't have what it takes to make it in the outside world," he said.

---

[3]Different psychics trained in different systems will "see" auras differently, because after all, we create our reality according to our beliefs. Even in John's system, pictures are just one element of reading auras, but sufficient for our purposes here.

[4]Although it is not necessary to be a conventional psychic or consult one to learn about oneself, it can be one way to go. John's expertise at aura reading provided Ellen with information she found valuable, much as his expertise as a lawyer might be valuable if she had a legal question. This happened in spite of the fact that at first, Ellen was rather skeptical of this "aura reading" business.

"No, she never said that to me, and never would," Ellen answered vehemently. "But she often said that of herself."[5]

"Well, you got the message," he offered. After a moment, Ellen acknowledged that she had taken on many beliefs from her model of femininity, her mother, and that this may well have been one of them.

As John continued, he saw another picture in the same area and commented, "Your father liked that about your mother; he liked that she didn't think she was good enough."

"Yes, I think it made him feel superior," Ellen agreed. She explained that the more her mother gained self-respect, the more her father drank and their marriage deteriorated. She started to describe their bitter divorce, but John was already reading another picture alongside the one he'd just seen.

"I see you as a kid playing Ping-Pong with a boy. You threw the game so he would win," he said slowly, as if he knew this sounded dumb.

Ellen's jaw dropped. "That really happened! That was so long ago, but it's stuck with me. He was an old neighborhood playmate; he had a new Ping-Pong table and I was a better player. But I'd gotten just old enough to realize that losing to a girl would be humiliating for him, so I let him win." The significance of this picture was its juxtaposition with the others. Ellen would describe herself as a

---

[5]This exchange is an important example of an appropriate psychic-client relationship. Never accept wholesale what any psychic tells you. Weigh it against your experience and instincts, and help the psychic to "fine tune" his or her impressions. In this case, John was grateful for the feedback that helped him to steer through his impressions, and Ellen was able to continue to follow along with his reading in good faith. (See chapter 11, Using and Developing Conventional Psychic Abilities.)

full-fledged feminist, yet her social convictions had not penetrated to some deeply held beliefs about being a "good woman," modest and sympathetic.

Then John suggested to Ellen, "Focus on your feet right now and tell me what you see." Ellen instantly remembered an old photograph she had found fascinating when she was a young teenager. It was of her mother when she was the same age, standing awkward and pigeon-toed before the camera. Staring down at her own inturned toes, Ellen saw how she had literally and figuratively adopted her mother's stance.

Moving to the hip area, John observed that Ellen was psychically nurturing both her husband and her children on the right side. The picture suggested to Ellen that she was reacting to beliefs from her mother's dilemma—that the cost of self-actualization was the break-up of her family. Ellen's commitment to her present-day family and her expectation that her success would trigger its dissolution meant that her deep self was going to have a hard time manifesting her professional aspirations, unless she changed her expectations.

In the throat and shoulder area, John picked up on a past life where Ellen had also been a writer, a male. "I can't tell exactly how, but you confronted someone who reacted with strong antagonism. He damaged your career. That experience is affecting you even now and making you afraid to take a public stand on your own original insights." Ellen had no personal recollection of this conflict, but she did have chronic problems with her neck and shoulders.

At the top of the head, John saw another past life. "You've got some kind of 'Vestal Virgin' stuff up there, a lingering belief that it's more spiritual to be feminine." Ellen's initial response was that male energy *is* all too likely to lend itself to cruelty and corruption. Then she realized that this belief would limit her; and that both male and female energy would be necessary to attain her objectives.[6]

SEEING THE SYSTEM

This extended reading demonstrates not simply how a belief may be held even in spite of other contrasting beliefs; but also how beliefs operate in an entire system, literally from head to toe. Beliefs are organic and operate interdependently, both psychically and biologically. We can access the system in a variety of ways. The important thing is to learn to work with beliefs in light of their scope and influence.

Once you begin to understand that beliefs are multidimensional—involving inner light, intellect, emotions and the physical body—it's easy to see that beliefs can't be separated into single blocks. Because of their intellectual training, John and other members of the Seth class tried to isolate beliefs—rather like fussy eaters who scrupulously consume first their peas, then their meat, then their carrots, keeping each portion separate on their plates. Just as all food mixes in the stomach, all ideas and experiences mix together in the aura. You may isolate your convictions intellectually, but at the body and other levels your beliefs are all mixed together.

John likes to tell the story of his Yankee cousin's visit to Georgia. Extolling the virtues of southern cooking, John allowed as how she really ought to try grits. "Okay," she agreed tentatively, "I'll try one."

---

[6]Typically, the kind of insights Ellen gained from her reading come gradually, over time. In order to make our point, we have abbreviated the reading considerably. Ellen reported that months later, she was still deriving benefits from this reading.

"You can't have one grit!" John laughed, and it's the same with trying to isolate beliefs. Beliefs don't exist individually, but clumped together. Together they constitute a sphere of availability for events and circumstances.

7 On Changing Beliefs

WHEN OUR FRIEND Annie was growing up, nearsighted from an early age, she became well known for her clumsiness. In high school, her habit of bumping into furniture, dropping things and otherwise "spazzing out" were an unending source of entertainment for her friends. She was still bruising herself weekly in mishaps with kitchen cabinets, car doors and staircases well into adulthood.

When she was in her 30's and suffering from fitness anxiety, she decided to take a ballet class. In just a few weeks, people started remarking on her more graceful carriage. Even Annie noticed that her posture was improving, but it took a while before she realized that somehow, the klutz spell had been broken. This not only changed the appearance of her shins from perpetual black and blue—it also changed her bearing in the world. She moved with a new equilibrium and assurance that benefited all her other activities.

Annie's beliefs about herself as a klutz changed indirectly, without her deliberately addressing her past experience and assumptions. Hers is an example of the kind of normal alteration that goes on naturally all the time. We are constantly inspired, altered, moved and transformed by experiences throughout our lives. Understanding this, the practical psychic simply makes more deliberate use of what has always been the case.

There are two steps to the practical psychic's approach to changing beliefs. The first is to identify them; the second is to change them by enlisting the deep self through practical fantasizing.

IDENTIFYING BELIEFS

When you want to investigate what beliefs may be operating in a particular situation, you can simply ask yourself—and your deep self—what's going on with you. "Do I have beliefs that are interfering with the fulfillment of my desires here? What are they?" However, with difficult issues your beliefs may not be so readily accessible.

One approach to knowing yourself and your beliefs better is to regard your experience as a mirror of yourself. We call this effect, "What You See Is What You Are" (WYSIWYA, pronounced "wi-see-we'ya"). As an example, let's consider a conflict that one couple of our acquaintance, Harry and Susan, used to have regularly.

Harry is one of those drivers who gets upset over the misconduct of other motorists. For years, he'd fume away as he drove, venting his hostility in honking and hollering. Susan would respond to his anger by trying to convince Harry that he shouldn't be so angry. She would helpfully point out that things weren't really so bad, that they weren't behind schedule, and so on. This only added to Harry's irritation, and that in turn added to Susan's.

It took years for them to surmount the problem, but eventually, Susan asked herself a provocative WYSIWYA question. Obviously, Harry was overreacting to other motorists; was there some part of her life where she was overreacting? She realized that, in her family as she was growing up, expressing anger as Harry would do was utterly unacceptable. This learned belief was dictating her response to Harry's anger, making her feel compelled to try and control Harry's behavior by trying to talk him out of his feelings. In other words, she was overreacting to Harry's overreacting.

Susan's insight and consequent change in attitude helped Harry change. He no longer had to deal with Susan's attempts to control his temper. He was able to realize that much of his anger at other drivers was over his inability to control *their* behavior. He realized that he'd picked up attitudes of impatience and urgency from his family as he was growing up. Ultimately, both Harry and Susan discovered problems that they *could* control, because those problems lay within their own belief structures.

WYSIWYA AND THE HALL OF MIRRORS

Harry and Susan's example illustrates several useful points about identifying beliefs. First, this "Hall of Mirrors" effect is most often found with those closest to us; however, because close relationships are so highly charged, they can also be the hardest to observe with perspective. It will be easier to maintain perspective if you remember that it doesn't matter who is right and who is wrong. The point is to usefully observe the reflections around you.

Secondly, just as a mirror reverses your image, reality often reverses the image of your belief; or, it may mirror your beliefs with exaggeration and distortion, like a fun house mirror. Often when you experience a strong negative reaction to someone, it is a signal. When you catch yourself thinking something like, "Boy, is that guy ever stupid," ask yourself if there is something going on in your own life where you're out of touch.

The WYSIWYA technique doesn't work unless you're resourceful and willing to suspend blame. Had Susan simply said to herself, "*I* don't act like a jerk in traffic," she would not have broken through her difficulty. Concluding that Harry acted like a jerk in traffic and she didn't, though true, was not useful in helping her solve the problem. What helped was to assume that Harry's irritating conduct was a clue to some behavior of her own. Her reaction wasn't the same as Harry's. His behavior was reversal and distortion of hers, as if she were seeing herself in a fun house mirror.

It may not seem fair that Susan's best strategy was to change her own behavior when Harry's was far more inappropriate, but it's always easier to change your own behavior than to force a change in someone else's. In this case, her change turned out to be the primary trigger in Harry's changing his behavior, so Susan benefited both by growing personally and enjoying the change in Harry's behavior.

Using the mirror technique, both Susan and Harry discovered beliefs affecting areas of their lives in ways they hadn't imagined. Beliefs and their implications are often overlooked or only partly apprehended. However, your conscious mind is a powerful tool to evaluate consequences. Use it as a feedback mechanism to understand beliefs that are giving rise to experiences, much as you can use your conscious mind to analyze the contents of a dream. The next exercise can help to get you started.

EXERCISE 8
LIFE COULD BE A DREAM

In this exercise, you treat reality—a specific incident, a recent day, or any portion of your life experience you choose—as if it were a dream. First, recount your "dream" by writing it down, talking into a tape recorder or sharing it with others. Then, interpret it. What does this reality/dream mean to you?

This exercise can be done in a number of ways. If you already keep a dream journal or have studied with a dream group, you can simply apply familiar techniques. If you have no usual approach to dream interpretation, you might try the gestalt approach. Imagine that every element of the dream/reality story—whether character, setting, object or other feature—represents a feature of yourself. Be each feature of the dream, and talk to the others. Fully explore what each might say if it could speak, really letting your imagination go. (There are many books on dreams that propose a variety of approaches. Consult the appendix for recommended reading.)

Your interpretation of this reality/dream is yours, whether you work on this alone or with others. How does reality reflect symbolically, dreamlike, the issues you have been dealing with? What beliefs underlie those issues?

THE ECOLOGY OF BELIEFS

Once you identify your beliefs, you will want to change some of them. But just as the relationship between living things and their environment is vital to survival, so is the ecological balance between your beliefs and your world.[1] John's experience as a callow youth is a cautionary tale.

After graduating from Harvard Law School, but before going to work, John spent a year and a half redoubling his spiritual studies in India, San Francisco and upstate New York. He learned to recognize so-called negative beliefs, and proceeded to throw away all the stuffy and uptight beliefs about how to make his way in the world. Up until that time, he had done pretty well using his parents' beliefs in hard work and adjustment to society's demands. After all, he had made it through Harvard Law School without its putting a crimp on his investigations into meta-

---

[1]Using the term "ecology" for this concept comes from Richard Bandler's *Reframing* (Moab, UT: Real People Press, 1982), pp. 50–2.

physics. Now that he had all the tools, he felt he would no longer have to conform to society's expectations, or work hard, or learn from the world. He had studied with the greatest teachers of the age and anyone who had the good fortune to hire him, he thought, would surely benefit from his unencumbered vision of cosmic truths.

Consequences came crashing in. Amazingly, people who hired lawyers weren't interested in metaphysics. They wanted employees who were devoted to researching and arguing cases. Whereas for John's first twenty-six years he had known nothing but success in any major undertaking, for the next several years he knew nothing but failure. His old beliefs, though weak and inadequate, had been serving a vital function in his personality. If he had known then what he knows now, he would have been a little less hasty in abandoning so-called negative beliefs.

Every belief you have, you have for a purpose. Every belief you form, you form because it is the best evaluation of reality that you can make at the time. Before you abandon any belief, take some time to figure out what positive purposes that belief serves.

Once you have identified a belief that's been causing you discomfort, use practical fantasizing to change that belief to a more advantageous one. Make sure your new beliefs include the advantages of your old beliefs while releasing the disadvantages. Here are three practical fantasies for changing beliefs. They don't have to be done together, but they are complementary and when done together, their effect is cumulative.

Exercise 9
Freeing Yourself of Your Past

In a very imaginative fantasy, you can "blow pictures" of events connected to the belief. As we explained in the last chapter, pictures are memory imprints, traces of experience. Blowing a picture is a way of vaporizing the effect of an experience. You do not erase your memory of it, but dissolve the emotional charge that the memory carries. This may be done as often as you like, since some pictures persist stubbornly. While you do this exercise, remember to be open to new insights.

The best way to blow a picture is to throw it into a golden, molten sun that will remove the energy from the memory. Then recycle that energy back into your aura as warm, golden, free energy. Know that the information from the memory will always be available to you, even though you've dispensed with the psychic charge that it used to carry.

In the case of Harry, the hostile motorist, he changed his hostility toward other drivers by blowing pictures from his early family life. Today, he still remembers how family members often reacted with anxiety, impatience and urgency to situations where none of these were necessary or useful. But these memories no longer grip him emotionally and influence his behavior.

EXERCISE 10
DISCARDING BELIEFS

Take a belief you wish to change and make it into a single representative picture, sound or feeling. Then, use your imagination to erase it. You might make it a photograph which you then hold under a shaft of sunlight, burning out or dissolving the picture. If it is an auditory fantasy, drown it out with the sound of powerful ocean waves breaking, or any form of "white noise." If it is a feeling you recall, temper it inside yourself. If it makes you feel stiff and cold, warm it by a fire. If it makes you feel stressed and upset, rock it like a baby.

For example, Susan might have taken the belief that "expressions of anger are never appropriate," and used her imagination to recount how she feels, sounds or looks when people around her get angry. Then she would dissolve that experience in her imagination.

EXERCISE 11
BUILDING NEW BELIEFS

In this fantasy, you picture yourself exercising a new belief in place of an old one. How would your life change if, instead of your old belief, you held a different one? How would it look, sound and feel? Who would be affected, and how?

Take your time with this one. Play with the probable differences as you go through your daily routine. As you imagine yourself exercising the new belief, notice changes in your body language, tone of voice, responses toward others. Let these observations continue to inform your fantasy. You can even act out the change in a little drama you make up, alone or with friends. This can bring your body, mind and aura into play. Eventually, you can go beyond fantasizing and experiment by trying out the new belief in small ways.

In Susan's instance, she might visualize, hear or feel what it would be like if Harry's automotive tirades did not disturb her. Then she might make it a point one day to arrive at a destination smiling, emerging slowing and calmly from the car.

MUTATIS MUTANDIS

As people discover how beliefs affect experience in ways they never suspected before, they begin to wonder about those beliefs that are beyond conscious retrieval.[2] Experiences from early infancy, or even past lives, are beyond the recall of most of us, yet they do affect us. Even though the source of some beliefs may be out of reach, the events they contribute to are manifested in your everyday life. Once you identify a problem, you can ask your deep self to make the appropriate adjustments without ever consciously remembering the childhood (or past life) experience.

Mutatis mutandis is a Latin phrase used by the legal profession and means generally, "to make the necessary changes." We use it in a kind of shorthand with the deep self, asking that it bring in additional information that might be needed, and that it help with the changes necessary for integration.[3] When you perform exercises like the ones above, ending with mutatis mutandis is a nice way of invoking the assistance of the deep self. Whisper it to your deep self/horse as you ride. Sometimes, it will seem that the deep self takes care of things as if by magic. But often, it takes more doing. Sometimes making the necessary changes will require further life experience.

There wouldn't be much sense in working with beliefs if they didn't increase your effectiveness or fulfillment. They do. Once you have identified any belief, you can use it to make enormous transformations, just as a small rudder can change the course of an oceangoing vessel. Once you tell your deep self which direction you want to go, it can assist in huge changes. However, a rudder would be ineffective in directing a ship that was stuck on dry land. Sometimes you will need a sea of experience to change your course.

---

[2]Actually, from one perspective, you create your own reality according to your conscious beliefs (see appendix II). Nevertheless, by using the mutatis mutandis technique, you do not have to make everything conscious to have it work out.
[3]See appendix III for a discussion of probabilities and how you can change your past.

THE HARDEST WAY TO
MAKE A MILLION DOLLARS

A surprising percentage of New Agers, in that first bloom of enthusiasm that comes from discovering that they create their own reality, decide that they are going to win the lottery. After all, all they have to do is become psychic enough to pick a winning number, or, for the more sophisticated ones, work on their beliefs so that they will increase the ones supporting prosperity.

This is another version of the "life is a trick question" approach, as if the purpose of creating your own reality were to spare you the trouble of living. Of course, there is nothing wrong with wanting a million dollars, but there is a sound mystical reason why it is easier, in the long run, to make a million dollars in gainful activity rather than in the lottery.

It is almost impossible to alter your beliefs in an experienceless vacuum. Therefore, the best way to change beliefs is to live your life. The very reason you are physical is that physical reality has just the right amount of structure for your needs. If you try to finesse reality and capture the benefits without experience, you're usually going to come up empty. This delusion, that the psychic world is a substitute for experience, comes up again and again. People go to psychics to be told whether the new man or woman they've met is the ideal mate for them. New Agers looking for a job think that they can psychically determine which is *the* right job and walk in off the street to that one happy, successful interview for their dream job.

Sometimes, as a practical matter, you can't get there from here. If your "ideal" mate showed up before you had had much experience with other possible lovers, you might not realize which qualities made that person ideal for you. Without a lot of different job interviews, you might not have a clear idea of what you wanted and what was possible, and you might not have the social skills to have a successful job interview with the ideal employer.

If physical reality weren't sufficiently challenging that it required experiencing it to obtain its fruits, it wouldn't sustain your interest. Not many people would choose to play tennis with an opponent, day in and day out, against whom they won every single point. The purpose of life often seems to be becoming successful at some particular goal, but it isn't. You don't really play tennis simply to win. The purpose is to have experiences and to learn how to fulfill the values embedded in those experiences.

There's a folktale about a very poor farmer who captured a leprechaun and demanded that the leprechaun give the farmer his pot of gold. Using his gift of gab to send the farmer digging hither and yon, the leprechaun attributed each unsuccessful attempt to his confusion about where he had hidden the gold. By the time the farmer had dug up his entire farm, he was so exhausted that the leprechaun slipped away. After resting, and cursing the leprechaun, the farmer decided that since his land was already dug up, he might as well plant the entirety and see if he could raise a crop on his self-plowed land. In a few short months, the formerly impoverished farmer had a bountiful crop which he sold for his own little pot of gold. At that point, the leprechaun returned and explained that the farmer had had a pot of gold in his farmland all along, but had been too shortsighted to use his land to its full potential.

8 The Power of Beliefs in Practice

IN THE FIRST CHAPTER of this book, we explained how the practical psychic is perpetually balancing contradictory ideas. It is a paradox, but a true one, that your power is both limitless and limited. It may be possible for you even to walk on water, yet impossible for you to get your spouse to put the cap back on the toothpaste.

Techniques for meditating, visualizing and raising your consciousness have become well known, but a fundamental question underlies their application. What about the interface between these practices and the conduct of everyday life? Theoretically, there is no limit to the effects of these transformative practices. Practically, there are. In this chapter, with examples from real life experience, we hope to illustrate the power of beliefs as they operate in ordinary life.

CREATING VS. CONTROLLING REALITY

A common observation made by New Age students is, "If I'm creating my own reality, why aren't I doing a better job of it?" Or, to put it more bluntly, "If I'm so powerful, why aren't I rich?" (or thin, or famous, or otherwise fulfilled). The question holds the answer. Seth did not say that you command, dictate or decree your reality. He said that you CREATE it. Even if your desire is strong and your expertise exquisite, you won't always succeed at creating the reality you intend. A champion tennis player can't hit every single tennis ball exactly where he or she wants it to go. "Magic" Johnson doesn't make every basket.

Many of the Seth class members assumed in the beginning that since you created your own reality, you could control it easily, and that you could get each and every thing you wanted. This misapprehension led to foolish approaches to life and sometimes devastating guilt when difficulties were encountered. John's desire to become both psychic AND practical originated during this early reckoning.

It eventually became obvious that such control would not only be impossible, it would be ludicrous. Mastery over one's experience would make life as pointless as those tic-tac-toe games where both players know the strategy and tie every game.

Generally speaking, there are four basic elements in the game of life which make it impossible to control. They are:

1) the rules of the game;

2) the complexity of the game;

3) the meaning of the game;

4) the spontaneity in the game.

As a practical psychic, developing some feeling for practical limitations means you can begin to understand when to strive for solutions, and when to relax and go with the flow.

The Rules of the Game

Being born on earth means we follow certain rules. Our physical reality, for example, takes place in a time scheme where the only moment we have is now, with yesterday gone and tomorrow not here yet. Such rules are like the rules of a game, somewhat arbitrary but with an internal coherence and logic that makes exciting dramas possible.

In the game of tennis, players are allowed to hit the ball after it bounces once. If everyone agreed, the rules could be changed to require that all balls be hit before they bounce. But given our physical limitations, such a game would be too demanding. Similarly, we are told, there are dimensions of consciousness in which time as we know it does not exist. For those of us who are human, however, such dimensions would be too challenging.

We do have rules—such as gravity—that we all agree to follow. Ultimately, however, even rules such as the laws of physics are beliefs, and can be dropped by skillful individuals. Dropping such rules or beliefs is extraordinarily difficult. More importantly, since such rules have a purpose, it is usually wise to accept them. There is the story of the Buddha coming upon a yogi of great repute and asking the yogi just what he had accomplished with his decades of meditation. The yogi replied that he could now miraculously walk across the river. The Buddha replied that to get across the river, there was a boatman who would charge only a few cents. The practical psychic, like the Buddha, concentrates on practical goals.

RULES THAT CHANGE

It is a great skill to know which rules are easier to follow and which are easier to change.[1] Rules based on social beliefs can and do change as society's values and circumstances change. Until a few years ago, for example, it was widely believed that all men were biologically and spiritu-

---

[1]See the next chapter on impulses for how to develop that skill.

ally ordained to earn a living to support their families; and that all women were biologically and spiritually ordained to nurture their families. Members of both sexes awoke to the discontent of such limitations, and now many men and women feel entitled to share both financial and caretaking responsibilities for their families. Both social and personal beliefs had to undergo change for this to happen, and most of us are still struggling with what it means to be a man or woman free of these stereotypes.

Personal beliefs can be the easiest rules to change beneficially, but not if one omits self-encounter in ordinary life. Suppose, for example, the yogi who learned to walk on water was attracted to a mystical path because he wished to escape the difficulties of life. Instead of escaping, he could have engaged in ordinary experience. This would inevitably have led to changes in personal beliefs, and he would have penetrated the meaning and values of life more deeply.

That levitation may be possible is important to know, but not for the practical purposes of crossing rivers. Rather, it allows us to begin to get a sense of the vastness—indeed, the limitlessness—of our freedom. Understanding our limits empowers us by preventing us from wasting energy on silly or dangerous approaches. Understanding our limitlessness empowers us by keeping us from quitting prematurely.

THE PRACTICAL PHYSIQUE

Let's look at a real life practical situation. Lots of us are unhappy with our weight, usually because we weigh too much. The usual strategy for change is a regimen of diet and exercise. On the other hand, many who have heard that they create their own reality decide that they are going to create one in which they can continually gorge themselves and never gain more than their ideal weight. Both these approaches have serious shortcomings. Since your beliefs create your reality, you are the weight you are as a result of your beliefs.

Take Ken, for example, who would succeed in the beginning of his conventional efforts to lose weight, but then would stall. After zooming up and down in weight for years, he joined John's class and began to learn about beliefs. After some prolonged introspection, he discovered a fundamental and stubborn belief that he's a more powerful male, more of a real man, if his girth is substantial. Numerous supporting beliefs, such as those from his days as a high school football player, would always sabotage his attempts at weight loss.

After a promotion at work, when he realized he was adding pounds to match his weighty new management responsibilities, Ken began to work on his beliefs in earnest. This was a long term alteration that involved many levels of change, because eating involves a whole system of beliefs. But Ken attributes much of his success to pinpointing the beliefs that distorted what "enough" is. These included, "Food is the best reward." Whenever something was going well, he would have to eat whether he was hungry or not. "It's sinful to leave food on your plate," was another one. He would routinely overfill his stomach when his body was no longer hungry, thus enlarging both his stomach and his appetite. Alerting himself to these beliefs was a turning point in changing his habits.

Note that Ken did NOT work on developing a belief that no matter how much food he consumed, he would stay slim. Some people have tried this and failed. Eating, at its most fundamental level, ties into what it means to be a creature on the planet Earth. If your idea of pleasure is to be able to gorge with no sense of harmony with your body and the earth, you will probably never be both slim and satisfied.

Enjoyment and pleasure in eating are part of what physical experience is about. Ultimately all life is fed and supported by All That Is. Eating is an externalized "symbol" of that deep, mystical, supportive relationship. The more you can enjoy eating in balance and harmony, the more "full-filled" you will feel. But if your idea of enjoyment and pleasure are bloated, you will find yourself bloated.

The point is two-pronged. On the one hand you have more freedom to eat what you want than most people realize. If you feel like eating mostly sweets one day, then go ahead. That's the freedom that you have, and life is set up to work with an extraordinary freedom and grace. On the other hand, if you think that creating your reality means being totally out of touch with the needs of your body, then you're probably going to be disappointed.

THE COMPLEXITY OF THE GAME

Two competent players will always tie in a game of tic-tac-toe. However, no one, not even the best chess player, is absolutely able to control the outcome of a chess game. The strategic and psychological implications of most moves are too far-reaching to understand completely. Needless to say, life is richer and more complex than a chess game. And the implications of your beliefs are often astonishing.

Let's take an example that bedevils many women in our culture. Laurie has always wanted a relationship with a strong and warmly caring man. Yet, in a continually self-defeating pattern, she has perpetually found the men in her life to be overly aggressive, and even downright nasty. Are there no kind, strong men out there, she wondered?

Through examining her beliefs, Laurie acknowledged that dominating men seemed more attractive and exciting, so she went to work on changing that belief. However, even then she continued to discover herself interested in men whose hard edges ended up causing her pain. Her difficulty was caused by beliefs that did not appear to be pertinent, but were. Laurie believed, as many do, that the world is a very cold and cruel place. Furthermore, she felt certain that men were better equipped to cope in such a world than she was. Therefore, the basic message Laurie kept sending to her deep self was, "Don't leave me defenseless against a cruel world! Send me a mean s.o.b. who can wield a knife if he has to!" Ironically, a man with a character strong in hostility and aggression would eventually display these traits toward Laurie herself. Every relationship involves conflict. A man who habitually reacts to threats violently cannot be expected to work through such conflicts calmly. Laurie's knife-wielding s.o.b. would inevitably attack when he felt threatened in conflict, even with the gentle Laurie.

The world is a rich and complex place in which the events that occur do not always arise self-evidently from the choices we make. Laurie's story is a good illustration of the complexity of the game of life and how we create our reality according to our beliefs. We do make the choices, and those choices do determine the outcome. But just as it takes time for babies to learn how to focus their eyes and coordinate their hands, it takes us time to learn how to coordinate and understand the implications of our choices and beliefs.[2] And one of the practical uses of understanding the complexity of the game is to release yourself from unnecessary guilt when you "fail."

---

[2]See appendix II: On Conscious Beliefs.

GUILT COMPLEXITY

One of the hardest things to deal with once you learn that you create your reality is guilt over "failures." A poignant example occurs when New Agers are confronted with a diagnosis of serious illness. Often the sufferer and friends alike will question why the patient gave him or herself the disease. "If I create my own reality," the sufferer demands to know, "how could I fail in such an unpleasant way?" And how can anyone heal under a cloud of self-blame?

The implications of the choices that go into developing a serious illness, or whatever problem bedevils you, are often difficult to understand. Once you realize this, you can begin to dispense with false guilt. Guilt is only useful to trigger changes. When you make a mistake, your pain will lead you to make changes naturally, but holding onto guilt is not helpful.

Understanding that the beliefs we hold structure the reality we experience will greatly speed that process of change, but it will not bypass it. Not even the powerful tools of the practical psychic can guarantee that everything will proceed perfectly. In this society, to know and understand something implies that you will be able to control it. But that's not the way it happens in the psychic world. There is no level one ascends to where everything works out flawlessly.

Seth used the metaphor of an infant clumsily knocking over blocks and crying without understanding that he was responsible; eventually, the child learns sufficient coordination to avoid doing so. In much the same way, we lack the ability to coordinate and understand the full implications of our acts. You wouldn't expect a baby to feel guilty for knocking over blocks. It makes no more sense to indulge in recriminations and useless guilt when you fail to understand how to create the reality you want. Learning how to coordinate and appreciate the implications of your beliefs is part of the reason you are physical.

This leads to the second point about dealing with guilt. Failure, even painful failure, does not mean that you are going backward. Sometimes you will skillfully create impediments in order to learn lessons of profound meaning. For example, how could you ever learn real patience without having to wait "too long" for something very important?

Furthermore, your experience cannot be compared to anyone else's. As you become deeper and more perceptive, belief conflicts that previously were not important enough to cause a problem may start to do so. Of course, as you become deeper and more perceptive, the insights and abilities you have been developing equip you for coping and also lead you to greater pleasures. Although we have been focusing here on the negative, the overall meaning of the game is very positive.

THE MEANING OF THE GAME

Since you live in the physical world, you cope with and create physical experience. The meaning and value of life are carried within your experience of physical events. However, the meaning isn't the physical event itself. By way of example, money is valuable for the things it can buy, for the ego-gratification it brings, for the freedom it gives, or for the good it can do. But money isn't valuable in and of itself, unless you are a coin collector.

Physical events are containers for meaning, much like a cake pan holds the batter. You can put your batter into a square pan or a round one, or in several pans. Different pans will affect the appearance of the cake, but will have no effect on the taste. However, a pan of some sort is required for baking your batter; you can't just pour batter into the oven. Similarly, since we are physical, we require physical events to contain our meaning and values in a structure we can understand and cope with.

The deep self uses physical events flexibly and in cooperation with other life on the planet. We are all joint tenants of our reality. You may think you can only get the experience you want in a specific physical event, but in subtle ways, the deep self can mix and match events for an overall experience. As an example, we'll use what is perhaps the most common and challenging of shared experiences—marriage.

One of John's students, Al, asked, "What if I believe in prosperity and my wife doesn't?" You could replace the word "prosperity" with any number of other issues that couples differ about; the underlying question is the same: "How can I fulfill my values in my relationship when my mate does not share them?"

Such questions call up some basic conditions of relationships. First of all, you cannot control someone else's behavior or values. By the same token, someone else cannot control yours. In addition, much depends upon your being open and flexible to possibilities for fulfillment that may differ from what you have imagined. It's important to understand that the underlying value is what is really fulfilled; the particular physical experience for that fulfillment, like the cake pans, may take any number of forms.

The possibilities for Al, who believes in prosperity, and his wife Nora, who does not, are numerous. The probability of any particular event would depend upon the couple's other beliefs. It may be that Al attains what he considers to be prosperity, while Nora does not share his material contentment. That is, each may have a different subjective perception of their objective net worth. Or, their objective experiences may in fact differ. His professional fortunes may soar while hers never get off the ground.

As in any situation, Al could work on his own beliefs. He could begin by searching out new approaches and new areas of mutual satisfaction. Or, he might use the mirror technique to ask himself, "Well, Nora believes in scarcity around money. What do I believe is scarce?" Whatever he does to work on his own beliefs and attitudes can have a direct effect on the problem. In holistic theory, change in any part of a system affects the rest of the system. Therefore, a change in Al will influence the marital system, and may even increase the likelihood of Nora's making a favorable change.

In the most extreme situation, if Al felt he absolutely must share prosperity with a spouse, and Nora could not accommodate him, they might give up on their marriage and look for other, more fulfilling partners. Using beliefs, you have an extraordinarily powerful tool to influence others in the direction you want, but if they do not go in that direction, your efforts are not wasted. If you retain your flexibility, your deep self will cook you up a sweet dish somewhere else.

THE SPONTANEITY IN THE GAME

Seth constantly emphasized the value of spontaneity and play. But spontaneity can be frightening. As Theos, a teacher channeled by our friend, Dianne Kelleher, so aptly stated, "Everyone wants to be spontaneous, they just don't want surprises." Our whole Western scientific culture is based on the premise that absolute laws govern events, that the universe runs like a clock, step-by-step in an utterly predictable fashion. Fortunately, that's not the complete case. In a manner beyond the ability of our intellects to understand, the universe itself contains surprises. Seth states that without the creative imbalance built into all reality, life and meaning would be impossible. There is no level of consciousness at which surprises cease. They exist even for All That Is.

There are aspects of every event that act like a kind of Mexican jumping bean, capable of hopping in and of itself in any direction, which cannot be controlled or predicted. There is always a dynamic balance between predictability and unpredictability, so you're not left helpless in a senseless world. However, controlling your reality would require absolute predictability.

The practical power of beliefs is not in controlling your reality—it is in integrating your infinite potential with your practical limits. You CAN create your reality more successfully and more playfully, and there are infinitely more resources available to you than our culture normally acknowledges or uses. That is what this book is about. Sometimes, however, you will be severely challenged. In such circumstances, it doesn't help to rail at fate or your own shortcomings. In the words of the poet, "Everybody must get stoned."[3] Still, the resources are always there to fulfill your purposes. "Life is a promise that is meant to be fulfilled."[4]

As a practical matter, you cannot be both a winning jockey and a champion sumo wrestler, but your life can be rich and meaningful when you try to be one or the other— or an ordinary citizen. If you understand both your freedom and your practical limitations, you can develop strategies to determine when to strive to change the very rules of the game and when to go with the flow. How do you tell which you should do in a particular situation? The answer is in the next chapter, which discusses impulses and how to use them.

---

[3]Bob Dylan, "Rainy Day Woman No. 12 & 35" (Dwarf Music, Co., 1966). A young reader was uncertain of this allusion. We mean, as Dylan did, that everybody experiences failure, pain and/or rejection.
[4]Also "Theos," channeled by Dianne Kelleher, in personal communication to the authors.

9 Impulses: The Path Rising Up to Meet Your Feet

IMPULSES, THOSE SPONTANEOUS desires to go for a walk or take an unaccustomed way home, are the simplest and most delightful of all the tools of the practical psychic. An impulse is a psychic meteor, a flare of light where your deep self meets your conscious self. As you learn to follow your impulses you will find your true power, creativity and playfulness—what Seth called "natural grace."

However, impulses can seem scary because they operate in a different logic, and have different purposes than those you usually think are important. Braving such fear is worthwhile nevertheless, because following your impulses will eventually hook you into an entirely different, more inclusive way of thinking and using your intellect.

CONVENTIONS OF REALITY
WESTERN CIVILIZATION IN THREE PARAGRAPHS

Since the 16th century, we have used the intellect in increasingly narrow and structured ways—ways of enormous power, but no heart. Beginning with Galileo, Descartes and Francis Bacon, official patterns of thinking were based on physical proof. The official function of intellect in the West became to divide and conquer, to dissect and control. This limited application of intellect actually had its beginnings even further back.[1]

A foundation of Western thought is Aristotle's Law of the Excluded Middle, which first stated that a thing was either true or false. Ever since then, procedures for inquiry, for gaining and validating knowledge, have been grounded in the rules of a logic that insists a thing must be either true or false. The Scientific Revolution simply applied that true-or-false criterion to ever tinier portions of reality. Slicing up nature in order to study it, and then figuring out how to control it, became the basis of Western progress.

Western scientific inquiry seeks to exclude values and emotions. Excluding value and emotion allows the impartial study of phenomena as discrete, lifeless things, separated from their holistic context. But in the practical world, there is more than can be sliced, studied and produced. There are values and emotions that are both true and false, values and emotions which shift constantly without following palpable laws. You might take a moment to find a couple of examples in your own life. For instance, questions such as, "Do you enjoy your work?" or, "Is your marriage satisfying?" will often provoke a yes-AND-no answer.

INCLUDING THE MIDDLE

Impulses spontaneously integrate values and emotion with intellectual thought. This is what may seem frightening about impulses—they are not task oriented or success

---

[1]We are not arguing that the Greeks or the 16th and 17th century philosophers were wrong, evil, or stupid; just that these approaches don't work for the practical psychic. We are necessarily simplifying the issues here. For a fuller understanding, see the books about science and new ways of thinking listed in Recommended Reading.

dominated. They work toward pleasure and creativity.[2] Impulses do have their own automatic direction toward greater overall success, for without some measure of success you cannot be creative and experience pleasure. But the successes are secondary. Your love of (and engagement with) life is primary. Impulses may at times take you away from what you think should be your goal. But impulses present you with your natural path, the path that rises up to meet your feet.

"The heart has its reasons which reason cannot know," said the 17th century mathematician Pascal. His eloquent insight was meant to offset undue reliance on rationalism and logic. For the same reason, the reasons of your impulses cannot be followed by your ordinary "reason" or intellect.

THE NATURE OF IMPULSES

Impulses can be described as inducements to pleasure, to the reasons of the heart. That pleasure comes from the intersection of your private reality, what you think of as your personality, with the deep self. You may or may not tingle with pleasure, but you will feel anything from a soft wish to a great drive to act. Usually, impulses come in small sizes, simply as pleasurable ideas that occur to you. They come with the feeling that you want to do this, that it's appropriate and right.

Impulses may seem to you spontaneous and arbitrary, but you must understand that you have already been processing, playing out, choosing probabilities quite con-

---

[2]Sometimes an impulse will have strong unpleasant aspects as, for example, when the impulse is to avoid taking an airplane on which you have already bought a ticket. But the impulse is telling you where your pleasure lies—in not taking the trip.

stantly, but in ways you don't recognize. In sleep, for example, your dreams are very much in the business of working through scenarios and possible actions and outcomes. They are fast and immediate—no need to wait for the heavy material world to sluggishly conform itself to the choices you're experimenting with. In sleep, you are a supercomputer, tabulating exponential probabilities.

As we have said, an impulse is a psychic meteor, flaring momentarily into your attention. It brings awareness of appropriate action from the myriad of possible actions.

THE PRACTICAL IMPULSIVE

Modern philosopher Morris Berman, in his book *The Reenchantment of the World,*[3] eloquently argues for a view of the world that's open to its mystical, enchanted nature. To avoid foolish gullibility, he proposes the development of sound rules of the heart, which he labels "cardiac algorithms." These should complement the rules of the head. You don't abandon Aristotle's 2,300-year-old intellectual tools, but use them together with the heart.

Thus we are not suggesting that you act irrationally or destructively. "What if," you might ask, "I have an impulse to shoot my boss? Does following my impulses mean that I should shoot him?" Of course not. Because impulses are not governed by true-false rules, you do not have to take them literally. But the impulse might mean you should plan to move to another job, or talk to your boss, or consider a number of other alternatives.

The bulk of your impulses will be small, spontaneous desires that you can simply note and follow without adaptation. It is a good idea to get into the habit of following these to gain experience with the nature of impulses. Then

---

[3]Morris Berman, *The Reenchantment of the World* (New York: Bantam Books, 1984).

when an impulse that may involve risk does occur, you will have an experience bank to draw upon. The idea is not to dispense with thinking. You want to evaluate your impulses, but you want to integrate this thinking with your heart.

How to Explore Impulses

When an impulse strikes you, welcome and examine it. Is there an emotion behind it? Own that emotion and understand it is yours. For example, suppose that you have an impulse to hurl something at your spouse. Obviously, this is another impulse you should not enact, but don't ignore it either. Investigate the impulse. What's the feeling behind it? Irritation? Loathing? Fear? Follow that emotion and find its source and meaning. You will be discovering more about your self.

When there is relatively little at stake with an impulse, go ahead and act on it. For example, if you are driving somewhere in no particular hurry, and you have an impulse to take a new route, give it a try. Note the outcome of following your impulse. Did anything happen as a result? Perhaps you got lost, or came upon a beautiful view. Was there personal meaning in the outcome? What might finding your way out, or having a breathtaking break, have to do with your life in general?

Even when an impulse seems to come from nowhere, your thoughts and feelings are part of your experience. Impulses carry an emotional charge. Practice feeling this when you take note of an impulse.

Eventually, this becomes fun. You can program yourself to notice impulses the same way you can suggest to yourself that you will recall your dreams. Then when you catch an impulse, take heed. Follow the two rules of 1) exploring your impulse emotionally and intellectually; and,

2) following your impulse if possible. Enjoy your experience and reinforce it by suggesting to yourself that this will happen again.

MORE GUIDELINES AND PRACTICES

Be gentle with yourself and your impulses. Don't leap upon them and worry them like a puppy with a stick, or berate yourself when you think you've missed one. If you are uncertain what is a "true" impulse, that is okay. Experiment with anything that might be an impulse. Follow some, choose not to follow others, but always review the outcome. That way, you will build a reservoir of experience and become more adept at recognizing "true" impulses.

Remember that life is not a trick question. The object here is simply to notice your impulses. Eventually, paying attention to impulses will inform you about their nature and use. You will have enough experience in your reservoir to rely upon.

There are, of course, many other means to discovering your larger self. It may be that you record your dreams and discover in them curious but amazing feats of consciousness. It may be that you become more sensitive, more psychic, more enlarged through meditation. But impulses are the most immediate, most accessible demonstration of your intersection with your deep self.

IMPULSE PRACTICES

You might catch a glimpse of a meteor by accident, but you are far more likely to see one if you set up a lawn chair and spend some time gazing at the night sky. And so this chapter ends with suggestions for becoming aware of impulses when they happen to you—to figuratively set out your lawn chair.

1) Have an Impulse Day. For one day, pay attention to every impulse and follow as many as you can.

2) Pick one kind of impulse you feel is safe to follow. For example, decide that whenever you have an impulse to call a friend, you will. This is a good approach for those who find impulses somewhat scary.

3) Pick your scariest impulse of the week and brainstorm as many different ways as you can to act on the impulse, or part of it, safely. Have your friends join in if you like.

4) Choose not to follow an impulse, then see what happens. Notice if any connections appear between later events, pleasant or unpleasant, and your impulse.

5) Follow an impulse that seems not to make sense, but doesn't carry significant risk. Follow it literally. For example, suppose you have an impulse to shop in a store you've never gone into because the prices are so extravagant. Try it! You may find an appealing item has been marked down; or that something very precious is worth making room for in your budget; or that the clerk there puts you in touch with a sense of prosperity; or that you frankly don't care about such extravagances.

You will find as you become more skillful at recognizing and interpreting impulses that you can follow them more and more often, and have more and more fun doing it.

10 Aphorisms for the Practical Psychic

THERE ARE LOTS OF points of practical know-how for the practical psychic that can be explained simply. We have collected many of them in this chapter with easy-to-remember handles. These aphorisms proceed logically, and some people enjoy reading straight through them, like a full-course meal. Others prefer to snack on them. We invite you to partake in any way you like.

1. *Could the Buddha win at Wimbledon?*
As you gain expertise as a practical psychic, understand the relevance and limits of psychic abilities and spiritual illumination. Even transcendental illumination does not automatically translate into specific skills. If you are looking for a lawyer, don't go to a psychic, go to a lawyer. Likewise, don't expect that just because you become psychic, or become illumined, that you will be able to program a computer or prepare a soufflé without any training.

2. *Even Leonardo da Vinci had to learn to mix paints.*
Nobody, not even a genius, starts out an expert. Even though Leonardo da Vinci showed extraordinary talent from an early age, he still had to learn the most basic operations of his vocation. Similarly, not even the most brilliant law student starts out as a good lawyer.

It will take time for you to become adept at every new task, new ability and new belief, but you can begin to get small benefits immediately. Use those benefits to credit yourself for your efforts, and remind yourself of your progress. Remember that expertise requires experience and experience takes time.

3. *You can't do better than you can do.*
Students usually hit a stumbling block somewhere along the way, and worry that they are doomed to failure. In fact, all practical psychics are venturing into private and, for each, largely uncharted domains; it's natural at times to worry that you're not doing it "right." The point is to trust the process. It is absolutely true that no two of us are alike, and that goes for being practical psychics as well. It is important to appreciate that your experience is unique in its timing and its qualities; assume that you will proceed as smoothly and successfully as you can.

4. *You can't finesse yourself.*
A finesse is a way of going around a problem, but you cannot go around yourself. You cannot avoid your own limitations. You can only grow through and out of them. In real life, people often try to go outside of themselves to prevent themselves from making mistakes. Agonizing over decisions, they go to yet another psychic or deal yet another tarot. The fact is that, for the same reason that you can't do better than you can do, you can't finesse yourself. Recognize and enjoy your personal consciousness with its limitations—and don't expect a psychic technique or authority figure to protect you from yourself.

The first time he ever met Seth, John was a student torn between becoming a lawyer or a psychologist. He put the question to Seth, figuring that this wise being would certainly offer special advice. And in a way, Seth did. He told John, "If you knew me better, you wouldn't ask me such a question."

Even if you try to turn over your authority to someone else so that you don't make errors, ultimately, the buck still stops with you. You have to decide who has real insight, you have to interpret what they say and evaluate how good a job they're doing. Finally, anyone dumb enough to want to take over your life for you is probably not going to do a very good job. In other words, however hard you try, you can't get out of exercising your own authority.

There's a deeper, more subtle point as well. The reason people want to exceed their own capabilities is so they won't have to experience who they are. They hope for some idealized reality instead. But there is no "highest and best" when it comes to the Self. This is why, ultimately, it is impossible to finesse yourself—you are meant to experience yourself. For these reasons, it doesn't do to berate yourself for your errors. Your errors were an accurate reflection of who you were at the time.

5. *Strive to strive no more.*[1]
This aphorism is meant to be ironic. You want to learn how to trust the growth that comes spontaneously—how to relax and go with the flow—but many people find that learning how to relax and go with the flow is hard work. There is, however, a part of you that knows what it is doing. You can learn to trust that part of you and strive no more. As Jane Roberts wrote in one of her poems, "Before I knew what breath was, my lungs were breathing experts."[2]

6. *A flower knows how to grow.*
Seth often reminded us that a flower knows how to grow,

---

[1]This aphorism was coined by Will Ives, John's dear friend and member of the Seth classes.
[2]Jane Roberts, *If We Live Again: or, Public Magic and Private Love* (New York: Prentice Hall, 1982), p. 168.

and this aphorism encompasses the preceding five. It has several important implications. Just as a flower knows how to grow, each human knows how to grow. Therefore, it is inappropriate for one person to tell another how he or she should develop. Also, just as a flower does not have to work at growing because growth is part of its nature, people do not have to work at growing. Furthermore, you cannot make a flower grow faster by tugging on its petals. Likewise, you cannot forcibly accelerate your own growth. However fast you are growing is fast enough.

7. *If three people call you an ass, get a saddle.*
Listen attentively to the feedback that others provide you. Then, weigh what you hear. Give more weight to the observations of those who are very close to you. The point is not that you should believe everything they say, but that they are giving you valuable information. Other people's perspectives are valuable. And if there is a consensus about something that seems farfetched to you—if three people call you an ass—understand that they are using their best description of something that is important to them. You might not agree with the terms they use or with their interpretation of the situation, but you can use the mirror technique described in chapter 6 to learn what information they do have for you.

Another way to describe this is "aggressive listening." It means that you grant to others the integrity of their perceptions, observations and responses. These will be unique to them, and may not have much meaning to you. However, listening aggressively means you exert yourself to reach for their understanding, then decide how it can be useful to you.

Some feedback doesn't come from other people. If two appliances break down, or you are in several fender-benders, consider the coincidence a signal or clue. Look toward the meaning of the events. In some instances, there may in fact be a cause and effect relationship. For example, suppose your brakes keep burning out because you ride your brakes a lot when you drive. It's definitely the case that your habit is causing your problem. But the deeper question is, why do you ride your brakes? What might that reveal to you about yourself? Again, look toward the meaning.

You may be able to discern meaning even when there is no causal relationship. The term "synchronicity" was coined by Carl Jung to describe those connections of time and meaning that appear to have no cause and effect relationship.[3] Any synchronicity, approached with an open mind, can provide a great deal of information.

8. *Avoid left-handed lessons.*
Southerners use a homespun phrase to describe the kind of compliment that kills. A "left-handed compliment" is really an insult, such as, "My, that dress is becoming—it hides your weight so well." People on a spiritual path can fall into a trap that John calls "left-handed lessons." This occurs when someone decides that he has experienced failure because he was just too spiritual for the situation. You will sometimes hear someone say, "Oh, I was just too highly evolved for that partner," or "I wasn't greedy enough for that job." While such remarks may contain some truth, that kind of self-congratulation can blind you to learning. It's fine to use your experience to help you learn what to avoid. What to avoid is a negative lesson, however, which doesn't require any character change on your part. It is a good practice to assume that any unpleasant situation holds at least some clue to how you might improve your character.

---

[3]C. G. Jung coined the term synchronicity and explored the psychic ramifications of meaningful coincidence in *Synchronicity: An Acausal Connecting Principle* (Princeton, NJ: Princeton University Press, 1973).

There is here, as in every other case for the practical psychic, a balance to be made. It is appropriate to be clear in your judgment about situations to be avoided, such as unsuitable partners. Consequently we are not suggesting that you overindulge in self-criticism; we are just reminding you to look for possible improvement in yourself.

9. *You do need more than love.*
In the 60's, the Beatles sang, "All you need is love," but that's not quite enough for the practical psychic. It is true that approaching the world with love can provide a very powerful perspective, and that perspective can take you very far. Nevertheless, reality is so vast that it cannot be fully engaged from any one perspective. Any event of substantial scope in your life will require several different perspectives.

Life automatically provides you with different perspectives as you travel through time. Night turns into day, winter into summer and youth into maturity. Purposefully working to cultivate several perspectives about large problems is a necessary strategy for the practical psychic. One way to do this is by working with others. Whether this is in the context of a metaphysical class, a dream group, or healing gatherings, group members gain from sharing experiences and points of view. Hooking up with others will help you find confidence in your own progress and acquire an appreciation for the diversity and breadth of psychic development. You will also be nourished by the warmth and support of fellowship.

10. *Aim for where you want to go.*
While teaching their son to ride a bicycle, a couple took him to a park, where the ground would be soft for the inevitable spills. However, there were a few trees in the area, which they cautioned the child to take care to avoid. Again

and again, as soon as the boy was up and pedalling, he steered his bike into a tree. His parents had centered his focus on the dangerous obstacles. They then had to teach him to steer toward where he wanted to go, and forget about where he didn't want to go.

Applying the "aim where you want to go" principle often seems simple. For example, it is a well known "rule" that affirmations, a form of verbal self-programming, should be phrased positively. Rather than repeat, "I want to escape from poverty," you are advised to say, "I experience abundance." However, it may be hard initially to avoid focusing on the negative when emotions are intense. Nevertheless, by repeatedly using practical fantasies of your goal and requesting help of your deep self, you will find attention gradually shifting toward where you want to go.

11. *Let happiness surprise you.*
Sometimes, when we are striving to accomplish or attain something, we become so fixed on the goal that unexpected and superior alternatives are ignored. Focusing clearly on your goal while remaining open to unforeseen improvements requires development of that dynamic balance which is at the center of becoming a practical psychic. Developing specific goals helps root your desires in physical reality. But at the same time, you want to retain flexibility so that happiness can surprise you.

12. *There is no highest and best.*
A common piece of spiritual advice is to ask for whatever is "highest and best." This affirmation can be helpful in retaining flexibility in your projections. However, it can also prevent you from manifesting anything, because there is nothing that cannot be improved upon. Instead, just ask for something "nice" to happen. That's good enough.

13. *The elbow bends one way.*
This aphorism is a Zen saying pertinent to the practical psychic. It points out that some structure is necessary to operate in physical reality. One might think that an elbow which bent in every direction would provide more freedom, and it would. But that greater freedom would be more than offset by the loss of the elbow's loadbearing efficiency. What is true of the elbow is true for all physical systems. You have to have some framework, some belief structure to operate efficiently in physical reality.

14. *The life you save may be your own.*
One of the most deeply embedded myths of American culture is of the self-made man. This myth overstates the power of the single heroic individual. Everyone needs help, most of all the practical psychic, who gets help from the deep self, guides and other psychics. The idea that you can succeed without assistance denies the spiritual fact that we are connected to and interconnected with one another. It is natural to seek and offer help. It is also possible to go too far in the other direction. Much of the older spiritual literature exhorts students to deny personal desires and seek only to serve. This also distorts the nature of reality. You cannot authentically serve another by denying your own desires. Furthermore, since helping is a natural human impulse, service is not antagonistic to your desires. Dr. Bernie Siegel reminds his readers that service is a privilege, not an obligation.

Finally, a deeper understanding of reincarnation and gestalt consciousness leads us to realize that our own growth is tied to the progress of others. In a very real sense, the stranger you help may well be a part of yourself so that, literally, the life you save may be your own.

The Buddhists pray for compassion because an understanding of compassion greatly enriches their lives. The Dalai Lama, in a deceptively simple statement in which each word is deeply meaningful, says: "Out of my experience, I tell my friends wherever I go about the importance of love and compassion. Deep down, we must have real affection for each other, a clear realization or recognition of our shared human status."[4]

15. *If a man has a staff, give it to him.*
In high school, a friend of John's told him about weird Zen people who spent time contemplating curious sayings called "koans." An example was, "If a man has a staff, give it to him; if he does not, take it away." Neither John nor the friend could figure out what this meant. But years later, John read the words, "You cannot lose what is yours," and suddenly knew the meaning of the koan. You cannot lose what is truly your own. You cannot be given attributes that don't belong to you. Therefore, the wise person "gives" to himself and others what they truly own, and "takes away" illusion.

16. *"I'd do anything—but change."*
Often when someone announces, "I would do anything to get X, Y or Z," John adds silently, "Anything but change." For if you don't have what you want, it's because your beliefs aren't sufficiently open. For you to get what you want, you will have to change.

Frequently, people turn to psychic techniques as if they were some mechanical process that will make their goal happen. This confusion is often encountered with techniques using psychic "energy," such as the ones described in chapter 12. Though the technique seems to focus different kinds of psychic energy in a "mechanical" way, at a deeper level the technique is really a sophisticated way of helping you encounter beliefs from several

---

useful perspectives. The practical psychic must take care to understand that psychic techniques only work to help you change yourself.

17. *You cannot untie a knot by pulling on it.*
Another way in which people neglect the need for true change and transformation is to try to use mere intensity to overwhelm conflicting beliefs. This is usually an ineffective strategy. Rarely is lack of intensity the problem. The usual difficulty in gaining what you want is a conflict of important beliefs. Using intensity to circumvent conflicting beliefs is like trying to put a square peg in a round hole. Pushing it harder doesn't help. You must use a different peg or change the shape of the hole. Your impediments are part of you. When your hair is tangled, you don't just jerk your comb through it; you carefully untangle it. Where you have tied yourself into knots, learn how to unsnarl yourself gently.

18. *The grim promise—you will succeed!*
"You will succeed," sounds like the nicest thing you could hear. But sometimes you just want to give up, period. Then to hear that you will succeed becomes a grim promise. For example, consider the alcoholic: learning how to sustain sobriety is something each alcoholic is eventually going to learn, this lifetime, the next, or twenty hence. Many an alcoholic would like a vacation from the disease. Some would consider committing suicide. However, there is no way out of learning sobriety, not even suicide, for the challenge will eventually have to be met and faced.

This is reason enough not to commit suicide. You created the despair that you now experience, but as long as you're alive, you have a structure available and you can work through it whether it takes you a month, a year, or a decade. Unfortunately, if you commit suicide, you not only have to deal with all the issues that led to your despair, but you also have to reestablish a structure in which you can experience that despair and work your way through it. So, while all choices are valid, and there is no special punishment for the suicide, it is not a skillful attempt at a solution.

Of course most of us don't intensively consider suicide. But we do despair. Understanding that you will succeed can help you calm down, prepare, and start work on the challenge you know you will eventually meet. Even your mistakes carry you toward success. If it were theoretically possible for you to make the worst possible decisions all the time, you would still grow in understanding so that eventually your goal would be within your grasp.

19. *Every story has a happy ending.*
The other half of the grim promise that you will succeed is really much nicer. A time must come when you have solved whatever challenge faces you. Furthermore, there will eventually come a time when you will understand that basically, you never made any mistakes, that your actions were always the best you could do, even when they were not necessarily the best you knew how to do.[5] Often from that future perspective, you will understand that what seemed like a mistake was really quite creative, given your limitations at the time. From that future perspective, you will be less concerned with the seeming success or failure and more pleased with heartfelt emotional intensity and psychic expansion. From the future perspective, you will view the event as a success.

Why not accept the fact that there will come a time when you view whatever you were doing as having been a success and give yourself a break in the present? As long

---

[5]This distinction is frequently made. The particular characterization here was adapted from a talk given by Dick Sutphen, editor of *Master of Life* magazine (Malibu, CA: Valley of the Sun Publishing Co.).

as you're going to view yourself as a success someday, why wait?

20. *Anything that can go right will.*
The universe is not neutral toward your struggles. Your deep self holds its infinite resources constantly available to you. Any favorable event it can manifest consistently with your free will and beliefs, it will. Furthermore, it has vast creativity and power. It actively supports your positive urges and aids in the elimination of negative beliefs—again, always consistently with your free will. You are always watched and aided so that anything that can go right will go right.

11 Using Conventional Psychic Abilities

WE MADE A DISTINCTION in chapter 1 between the practical psychic and the conventional psychic. We described a conventional psychic as one who has developed paranormal abilities and can consciously make use of them. We pointed out that practical psychic abilities are both more important and easier to use than conventional psychic abilities. Even so, conventional psychic abilities are marvelous tools when used wisely and practically. They are fascinating, fun and useful. Furthermore, it is becoming ever easier to become conventionally psychic. Seventeen years ago John had to travel to India, San Francisco and upstate New York to find teaching psychics. Now, every large population center has several, and the degree of access is growing.

However, as attractive as developing and using conventional psychic abilities are, people seem to have a lot of distorted expectations about what paranormal abilities can mean. It's important to consider how you will make use of psychic information. Whether you are thinking of consulting a psychic or using your own abilities for the benefit of others or yourself, certain general guidelines will help you.

ESP: EXTENDED SENSORY PERCEPTION

It may seem too easy to be true, but the nearest, and most sensible gateway to extrasensory perception is your normal sensory perception. In other words, if you wish to become more clairvoyant, first learn to look around you with more attention and care. If you wish to become telepathic, listen more closely. By heeding more of the information already available to you—body language, tone of voice, the content and context of what you see, read, and hear—you will find your senses naturally extending beyond familiar limits. And this development will be a far more grounded and wise one than if you had pursued extrasensory perception for the purpose of escape.[1]

One of John's most difficult experiences on his road to becoming a practical psychic was the dissolution of his first marriage. At a time when he was developing remarkably as a psychic, he neglected to pay adequate attention to his wife's emphatic complaints and signals of distress. He was shocked when she left. It took him a long time to understand that even a psychic has to pay attention to ordinary information. To those he teaches, John now cautions, "You will eventually be able to talk with beings without bodies, but when you talk to those with them, listen!"

Psychic ability is a natural ability. If you had a natural ability in tennis, for example, it would take time, practice and good coaching to develop into a good player. Hitting the ball into the service court might seem impossible at first, and if you didn't know others could do it, you might give up. The same is true for psychic development. So take time, practice, and get good coaching where you can.

BECOMING A CONVENTIONAL PSYCHIC

Everyone using this book can immediately begin using their practical psychic abilities, but conventional psychic

---

[1]Sheri Burrows, one of the most naturally gifted psychics John has ever met, introduced him to the importance of allowing extrasensory perception to develop from normal sensory perception.

abilities must be recognized and nurtured, preferably under the tutelage of a teaching psychic.

There are a number of systems of psychic development using different vocabularies, symbols or descriptions of psychic reality. To recognize and nurture your conventional psychic abilities, it helps enormously to have some belief system oriented toward the development of conventional psychic abilities.

There are two important points to understand about these belief systems. The first is that a psychic belief system which is appropriate for you can help you recognize, nurture and coordinate the new kinds of data and abilities you will be encountering. The second is that every system is simply a belief system that you must ultimately tailor to your own unique personality and experience. For instance, some people find the Tibetan and Hindu chakra systems utterly natural. Others are finding a Western philosophical system, such as Jung's archetypes and collective consciousness, more satisfying. Still others are drawn to shamanistic beliefs and practices. For practical purposes, all of these approaches—and many more—provide legitimate structures for sound psychic development.

Most important is the understanding that you are in charge of what you choose to believe and act upon. Consider that the word "heresy" is derived from the word "to choose." In an important sense, being a practical psychic means being a practical heretic. John tells members of his classes, "Here's what I work with, here's my belief system. Borrow it for now, but as you develop, develop your own." In his own development, John gained immeasurably from both the framework offered by Jane Roberts/Seth and from Lewis Bostwick's system at Berkeley Psychic Institute. However, John follows neither to the letter. Over time, he adapted those principles to his personal experience. He discarded what did not work well for him, polished what did and perpetually adds to this matrix.

Whether or not you use or subscribe to a specific program for developing conventional psychic abilities, keep in mind that there are practical guidelines to apply in any psychic situation.

USE YOUR OWN JUDGMENT

John once received a reading that was in every respect factually wrong. However, the reader's distortions captured an emotional validity and even though the statements were wrong, John derived much insight and benefit from the reading. Strange as it may seem, information may be very psychic and yet very wrong and useless, just as information that is not psychic at all may be very useful. The standard Western intellectual approach does not work when evaluating psychic information. In particular, when using the scientific method, one tries to establish the authority of laws which are inviolate. Once you know a law, you know what to do in every situation to which the law applies. Certain rules are established to determine whether a pronouncement is authoritative enough to be believed and followed. In the psychic world, there are no inviolate laws and nothing to be believed on the basis of authority. The most you can establish are useful patterns and sources of information which you find to be beneficial and useful.

Some people counsel that when you go for a psychic reading, you should be careful to disclose nothing to the reader. Only by being secretive, they say, can you tell whether the reader is psychic or not. The practical psychic goes into a reading openly and helpfully. Most psychic readings are better if there is give and take between the psychic and the readee. If you are confused about something, ask a question. If you disagree, say so and the psychic can clarify what is being said, or get back on track, or continue to disagree. Psychics are humans and readings proceed best where there is rapport. Don't worry that rapport will interfere with your ability to discern whether the information is from truly psychic sources. The source of the information is irrelevant. The value of the information is all that matters.

KEEPING YOUR SENIORITY

The principle of balance and harmony is particularly pertinent to psychic information. Never assume that psychic information is superior to other kinds of information. There is something very special about the ability to pick up things in psychic ways, but this does not mean that other means of gaining information or making decisions are less valid. If psychic abilities were that surefire, all psychics would be living off their lottery winnings.

Unfortunately, this is a lesson some people learn at great cost. We knew of one man who was uncertain about his stockbroker's methods of handling the money from a hefty insurance settlement. During this time, he consulted a psychic, who told him that the way to find trust was to give it. He took this to mean that he should trust the stockbroker, and lost hundreds of thousands of dollars. This incident is a dramatic example of what can happen. The man's instincts were on target—he did indeed feel suspicious of the broker—but he gave more weight to the psychic than to his own insight and common sense.

This story also illustrates one of the reasons why keeping your seniority is necessary. It's quite likely that the psychic never intended for the man to rely utterly on that particular broker. The psychic may have been suggesting that the man find a broker he could trust; or the psychic may just have been inarticulate and meant that the client, himself, was untrustworthy in some subtle ways and so must work on that before he would be able to trust others. Communication is an imperfect transaction; meanings are easily altered in translation and interpretation. Retaining your seniority will help you screen out miscommunications.

John emphasizes the principle he learned at Berkeley Psychic Institute: "Always remember that you are the senior partner in any psychic situation." This is true whether you are consulting a psychic or are in touch with a personal guide. Any individual—incarnate or otherwise—who tries to persuade you against your better judgment is to be avoided. You will also want to avoid ignoring advice prematurely. If the information offered seems wrong or off, you should query the psychic. But after you have done your part in probing the source, then you and only you must decide how and whether to use the information. There are a lot of good psychics around, so you needn't settle for anything less than your full bill of rights. You will always be personally responsible for your decisions, so it only makes sense to retain your seniority.

Sometimes a Psychic Approach is not Practical

Another way in which people distort the value of psychic information is illustrated in the example of the woman who once called John for help with her sister. The sister had just been beaten by her husband again, and the woman was hoping that psychic insight into the karmic relationship would help. John suggested that past-life or karmic information wasn't nearly as important to the sister's circumstances as seeking safety, treatment and documentation of her condition. John would be glad to help, but only after practical steps were taken to ensure the sister's safety.

In a lighter vein, consider this charming ceremony once conducted by a skillful channeler: each attendee wrote down a problem on a small piece of paper which the psychic then placed in a metal dish and set on fire. Unfortunately, the tabletop underneath the dish was wood and the ceremony scorched it. Just because the channeled entity was extraordinarily knowledgeable and loving didn't mean that it was paying attention to physical practicalities.

THERE ARE NO GUARANTEES

Psychics are not infallible, nor are non-physical teachers or guides. This can be a hard thing for many of us to accept. We are accustomed to assuming that worthiness and perfection go together; and many people deify nonphysical beings. It can be a great challenge to entertain ideas to the contrary. As a matter of fact, the true practical psychic regards the whole notion of a true-or-false, yes-or-no system of logical thinking as one of many approaches. It is up to each of us to derive what is useful and worthy from whatever and whomever we encounter, including psychics and guides. Bear in mind that there are disagreements on the astral plane. As above, so below—there is no such thing as one truth.

In another vein, John was once uncertain about continuing a legal case and consulted a guide about it. With the guide's suggestion that it was worthwhile to continue, John laid aside his fears of losing the case, proceeded, and eventually lost. Disappointed, he asked the guide why he hadn't been warned. The guide answered, "So, you want only things that are cast-iron certain?" It could have worked out, but it didn't. The guide pointed out that sometimes you need to stretch.

GUIDELINES FOR GUIDES

At one point in his psychic development, our friend Jerry opened up to some very high spirits and found it overwhelming and unpleasant. They seemed to come even when he didn't want them, and he found them too forceful in trying to overcome his "limitations." He solved the problem by refusing to deal directly with any spirit or guide, setting a boundary by stating that any being that wanted to communicate with him would have to be screened through his own higher self.

Jerry was happy with this solution and proud of himself for having dealt with the deceptive allure that psychic abilities can hold. However, he also complained of feeling increasingly isolated personally and socially, even as he made palpable spiritual progress. There seemed to be a connection between the way Jerry had handled his spirits problem and the isolation he was feeling in the ordinary world.

Jerry believed that the purpose of experience was to break through the ego, to destroy it, so that he could evolve to a higher state where he was perfect in his loving and never made mistakes. Feeling that way, he had several disabilities when encountering spirits. First, he was not able to exercise independent judgment because he felt his judgment was blighted with his ego, his fallibility and his lack of cosmic lovingness. Second, he felt a desperate need to hurry the process along so he could escape his presumed "lower vibrations." This left him fixated on sources of potentially greater wisdom and love. Even as part of his mind was broadcasting, "Go away, I just want to be human now," another part plugged in urgently, like an addict, because that portion felt so weak and needy. It is for just such reasons that this book begins with, and constantly repeats, the conviction that all life has purpose and meaning. We stress being natural. Then growth will handle itself.

Just as there are no boundaries to the self, there are no boundaries to a belief. The same belief that was operating when Jerry felt it necessary to protect himself from spirits was making him feel vulnerable when relating directly to ordinary people. But he didn't have to be perfectly loving or perfectly egoless to have fulfilling relationships with spirit OR human beings. Following suggestions for dealing directly with spirits from the clarity of his own seniority helped Jerry to feel decidedly more adventuresome and at ease, both psychically and socially.

PRACTICAL CHANNELING

There are several common misapprehensions that can obstruct the benefits of communicating with guides, or channeling. The first is the belief that channeled information comes straight from some high being's mouth to your ear. Any channeling is a joint artistic creation, an attempt of four dimensional humans to interact meaningfully with much greater dimensional consciousness. Information is therefore always filtered through the channeler's beliefs and abilities, as well as through language itself. This is true of both conscious and so-called "deep trance" channeling.

Another problem is the conviction of some psychics that they have touched the highest energy in the universe, or the best energy available. Because channeling is an artistic collaboration, the so-called level of the information or spirit being channeled is mostly irrelevant. When you look at a painting of flowers, you never worry whether the actual flower subjects were beautiful. You merely decide whether you like the painting. When you try to evaluate channeling, never concern yourself with where the spirit comes from, but with whether a particular piece of information is useful.

Such misapprehensions come from a fundamental misunderstanding of the nature and purpose of the universe and result in mistaken ideas about the potential for "perfection." They create fears of evil and of low vibrations, fears which can create bad experiences like Jerry's. As a rule, spirit beings are too wise and playful to cheat you out of your learning experiences, including your mistakes. Beings may give advice to the best of their ability, but will never disrupt your boundaries. Any entity, however high and grand, is a guest of the channeler.

Becoming Psychic
A Digression by Your Co-Author

In the beginning, this book was to be John Friedlander's contribution to New Age posterity. We decided to write together after John read a couple of articles I had written, and asked if I would be interested in collaborating with him. John had developed a practical approach to using metaphysical concepts in everyday life. He offered concepts thoughtfully, with a refreshing lack of craziness. I wasn't particularly interested in developing my psychic abilities, but I knew there was a mystical layer of reality that everyone accessed, "psychic" or not. John's secure practicality was just the ticket for those of us who are more ordinary, I thought.

So I was happy to let John be the psychic as I toiled to get his practical principles down on paper. Several months after we'd started on the book, however, John urged me to take his classes because they would provide me with more background. In the first class, I learned about chakras and meditated on them, and enjoyed the benefits of a kind of euphoric relaxation. This psychic work all seemed to be done in the imagination, familiar turf for me, so it was easy and pleasant. Eventually, we learned to hook up to a "psychic healing guide," which again seemed to take place in the imagination, but with the extra dividend that I could really feel a kind of subtle, "hummy" energy.

In a more advanced class, we were to meditate on and "read" the chakras of other people, which was something that I couldn't just make up in my imagination. And so, as I sat there mentally grunting to "see" something in a woman subject whom I did not know, I said nothing about what I was imagining. When we were halfway along, I was told to speak up.

"If you perceive something, you should go ahead and share it. Do you have an image?" said my coach.

"Well, yeah, but it's stupid. I'm sure it doesn't mean anything."

"You should at least give it a try."

"But it seems so dumb," I protested.

"What is it?"

"A map, of France," I said, my voice dripping sarcasm.

Our subject looked up at me and said informatively, "I speak French. I teach French. I'm leaving for France in two weeks."

After a stunned moment, I jumped up and yelled across the room, "Hey John! I'm psychic!"

That first experience was to be repeated many times as I struggled to discover the difference between imagining and perceiving, between expectation and actuality. A year later, I could not only do readings when asked to, but "channel" at will, either at the keyboard or vocally. It has become hard for me to think of being psychic as something different from being organic, or literate, or maternal. It's just simply part of what I am and do. John asked me to tell about my experience here, because it may help readers to understand their progress as psychics.

I don't aspire to become a "great psychic" and am consistently impressed by those, like John, who have developed this extraordinary talent. Yet, I have also learned that being psychic is infinite in scope and I look forward to exploring its limitless possibilities.

In the next chapter, we will introduce an extended meditation for manifestation. For many, meditation is the gateway to becoming more psychic, not so that you can make predictions of world events, but so you can improve the quality of your personal life. For us, this is the mystical practice of the axiom, "Think globally, act locally."

12 Manifesting What You Want: A Chakra by Chakra Meditation

IN THIS CHAPTER AND the next one, we will be concentrating on systematic, long-range psychic techniques for manifestation. The practical fantasies you have been using are excellent practice for these longer and more extensive meditations.

As we described in chapter 6, you create your own reality according to your beliefs, and those beliefs operate systematically throughout your psychic/biological system. In this meditation, we will use the chakra model of psychic biology to bring a desired belief into your reality.

Chakra (pronounced "chak-ra" or "shock-ra") is a very old word from Sanskrit meaning "wheel." The word has become more widely known in the West as the practice of yoga has become popular. The theory behind yoga is that the body comprises an energy system. What the Hindus call "prana" (energy) courses throughout the body, and the main trunk of energy runs vertically through the center of the body like a spine. Along this main trunk are seven major "chakras" or energy centers, which spin like wheels.[1]

---

[1]Usually a discussion of chakras is a discussion of psychic energy. The chakra system helps you to learn to identify and use different kinds of psychic energy. However, the concept of psychic energy is a misleading one. In fact, psychic energy is not energy at all, in the sense that most physicists would use the word. Mechanical energy can be described in mathematical equations that specify an

Figure 1. The locations of the chakras

exact range of results. Mechanical energy seems to exist objectively, outside of the object that it acts upon. Mechanical energy is a cause of events.

Psychic energy is called psychic energy because it sure as hell subjectively feels like energy. When you feel psychic energy, there seems to be varying intensities that can energize or de-energize. But at its deepest level, psychic energy is an inside, as opposed to outside, phenomenon. Psychic energy has to do with relationship. It is a subjective experience of the quality of your beliefs, and consequently how close or distant, intense or weak your relationship with other portions of All That Is is. This is a deep philosophical point, but it does have an important practical implication. It is not an effective strategy to try to overwhelm so-called bad energy with good energy. With physical energy, whichever energy is stronger will dominate. But psychic reality operates differently and subtly, and the very attempt to overwhelm negative phenomena energizes them. Instead of attempting to overwhelm, one properly uses psychic energy to clearly understand what one likes and doesn't like.

When you identify an unpleasant or inappropriate energy, change it by blowing pictures or using some other technique to change your beliefs. Thus

While studying with Lewis Bostwick at the Berkeley Psychic Institute, John learned to meditate on and read chakras. See fig. 1 on page 94. Each one of the seven corresponds to specific functions in the psychic biology. Before we begin, we want to briefly identify and describe each chakra. You may notice minor discrepancies among different psychics and writers about what each chakra means. The overview we are giving here is meant to be a general, rather than a highly specific, guide.

The *first chakra* is at the very base of your spine. This is the survival chakra; many perceive it as red, the color of blood and vitality. This is the center that grounds your physical reality. It is the site of the reproductive organs—the roots of generation and earthly form. It encompasses the most fundamental operations of physical maintenance and overall well-being.

The *second chakra* is located in the center of your belly, an inch or two below your navel. This is the chakra of sex and of sympathy. Some associate it with the color orange, a "healing" and creative color. It is mainly from this chakra that you experience the feelings of others, whether sensory, emotional or intuitive.

The *third chakra*, at the solar plexus, is your "get-up-and-go" chakra. It is the site of ego energy, that is, personal power, initiative and creativity. Its traditional color is yellow, with its associations of intellectual learning and clear thinking.

The *fourth chakra* is the heart chakra. At this center, the soul is said to take up its residence in the body. This is the site of at-one-ness, of your unity with others. It is usually

---

when you are changing your psychic energy, you are not dealing with some mechanical phenomenon; you are changing yourself. So be nice to yourself—don't treat your energy as a thing, or something alien imposed on you, but as a part of yourself to be experienced.

depicted as green, a soothing color denoting peace and harmony.

The *fifth chakra*, located at the throat, is the center of communication. This entails all manner of self expression, whether speaking, singing or listening to your "inner" voice. Generally associated with blue, this is also the chakra of telepathy and clairaudience.

The location of the *sixth chakra* is the center of the head, including an area that many call the "third eye." It is the center of all types of vision—physical, clairvoyant, aesthetic, prophetic. This is where mental pictures can be "seen" to become reality. Its traditional color is indigo.

The *seventh chakra,* also called the crown chakra, is located at the top of the head. This is where cosmic energy comes into the body; it connects you to the knowingness of the All That Is. Usually described as violet, this is the chakra of spiritual growth and self-realization.

As with everything else, the more time you spend learning and meditating on the chakra system, the more you will derive from it. The Chakra Visualization for Manifestation can be used even by the beginner, but first we want you to become familiar with your own system. The following Practical Fantasy will help you to get to know your chakras.

Exercise 12
Get Acquainted with Your Chakras

Place your hand on your first chakra and let its color suggest itself to you. Then ask yourself for a sound or tone that seems appropriate for this chakra. If possible, hum or sound that tone vocally. Then remove your hand from the chakra center. How does it feel? For example, does it seem warm or cool, swollen or empty, agitated or calm? This is a completely subjective exercise. If imagery or other sensory details come to mind, take note of them. If you quietly ask the reason for an image, an answer will usually come to you.

Now repeat this sequence with the other six chakras. Refer back to the descriptions if you lose track of them. Then, if you have time, repeat this sequence using your other hand. Note differences in your impressions with this hand. You may want to take notes on your exercise, during or afterward. Often impressions become more meaningful over time, and notes can prompt your memory.

Finally, understand that even though this may seem largely an exercise of your imagination, your perceptions are valid.[2]

THE CHAKRA MEDITATION

Before starting the Chakra Meditation for Manifestation, you need to decide what you want to project for. This may be trickier than it at first seems. We propose that you come up with something that is, above all, practical. It will also be simpler if you stick for now with a single objective. The example we will use here is that of Bob, a businessman and father who wants to quit smoking.

To begin, follow the same procedure you would for a Practical Fantasy—that is, find an uninterrupted place and time, and begin your relaxation. Then, imagine energy that exists outside and above you. Picture your objective forming in that energy above your head. Make it real in your mind by adding details.

2John got the idea for a chakra-by-chakra meditation from Petey Stevens, *Opening Up to Your Psychic Self* (Berkeley, CA: Nevertheless Press, 1984), pp. 214-5.

In Bob's case, he pictures himself as a nonsmoker. He thinks of all the situations in which he feels most uncomfortable and irritated about being a smoker, and then pictures himself untroubled and relaxed because he no longer smokes. He spends some time working on the details of what it will be like to be a nonsmoker. Now, having created for himself a Bob who does not smoke, he will use the chakra system to bring that Bob into his present body/mind.

Bring that objective down into the seventh chakra and KNOW it. This "knowingness" is a direct impression of the objective's timeless existence in your life, that every detail already exists and can be realized. Experience the rightness, confidence and assurance you feel at having made your projection a reality as if you felt them right now.

Bob imagines that nonsmoking version of himself being welcomed into his seventh chakra. He knows that he can swim without difficulty breathing; work at his desk without ashtrays around; enjoy himself after meals without a cigarette in his hand.

Now bring that image of your goal into your sixth chakra and see it. Recognize what it looks like to have accomplished it.

Bob begins by visualizing both photographic and x-ray images of healthy lungs. Then he sees himself exercising, playing basketball and looking fit and healthy on the outside as well as the inside.

Next, pull that projection down into your fifth chakra and communicate with it. Try to condense it into a single statement or affirmation that you can repeat to yourself.

Listening to his "inner voice," Bob gets in touch with his body's complaints about cigarettes. He then repeats to himself the affirmation, "I release all use of cigarettes and enjoy my free and healthy breathing."

Now bring that goal into your heart chakra, and be at one with it. Feel the affinity between your objective and All That Is. Feel the peace and harmony emanating from this development.

Concentrating on the whole chest area, Bob meditates on the cooperation between lungs and heart, breath and life. He recognizes that giving up smoking can optimize the alliance of soul and body.

Now, pull your projection down into your third chakra and realize the personal fulfillment that it brings you. Identify the ways in which it provides gratification and empowerment, and meets your values and standards.

Bob focuses on the pride and sense of accomplishment he anticipates once he has conquered his smoking addiction. He also imagines the praise and congratulations that will come from friends, co-workers and family—especially his children— and how good that will make him feel.

Next, let that objective sink down into the second chakra, and experience the emotion, the "gut feeling," of realizing it.

Bob concentrates on his second chakra and discovers the great relief that he will feel when he stops smoking. He acknowledges the denial, fear and shame he has felt over the physical and personal effects of his habit. He blows those fear pictures and replaces the pleasure he used to feel toward cigarettes with the pleasure of being freed from their effects. He experiences that pleasure as if it were happening in current time.

Finally, lower your projection into your first chakra and have the body experience it. Take a deep breath and let it out slowly. Let the objective suffuse your every cell, as a hologram contains the same image in each and any of its parts.

Bob meditates on his body and lets it tell him all the ways that tobacco interfered with its healthy functioning. He follows the path of his chakras and lets his head complain about dizziness, his throat about irritation, his chest about congestion and so on. He lets a green light from the center of the earth dissolve all these effects. He replaces them with images of health. He imagines every cell in his body to be clean and naturally robust. Finally, Bob asks his deep self to help him continue growing and make all changes necessary for the ecological balance of his beliefs.

Also, because Bob is a practical psychic, he does not limit himself to psychic techniques. Recognizing that his addiction is physical, he also consults a doctor, who gives him a prescription for nicotine gum which Bob keeps in his desk "just in case." He also contacts friends who have quit and who offer him support and useful information—the number of the local Smokenders representative, the name of an acupuncturist who has helped others to quit, and so on.

This technique can be used for all kinds of changes, not just physical ones. For example, you can use the chakra visualization to help get a job. Change is usually experienced on many levels, and you can help yourself to envision your goal by imagining its spiritual, biological, psychic, intellectual, psychological and visual effects.

This chakra meditation is based on a cycle of self in current time. The next chapter deals with long-term change in a context of time and nature.

13 Seasons: A Program of Manifestation

OFTEN, THE CHANGES we wish to undergo in our lives are long-term and far-reaching. Some transformations, like improving a marriage or changing careers, are just plain big. This chapter is devoted to an effective approach for such changes. More properly described as a program than a meditation, it breaks down your objective into a twelve part cycle analogous to the year. The rhythms of nature—of days and nights, of seasons, and of the planets in their paths—are universal and instrumental.

You will do more here than sit down, enter a meditative trance, and visualize, for this is a more ambitious undertaking. Although your goal may take less or more than an actual year's time and may start any time during the year, we want you to become exquisitely attuned to the cycle of time and change.[1]

Big changes weave in and out of your daily life, appearing in different perspectives as you gain experience. Such changes have no true beginning or end. The purpose

---

[1]In legal negotiations, often the most effective tool is to stop and decide what you really want, as opposed to what you want to ask for. This leads to deciding what you can live with, and allows alternatives to be sought which reasonably satisfy both sides. So before you visualize goals using chakra or any other techniques, it is most useful to sit down and decide what you want, brainstorm about alternatives and then look around and see all the potential resources you can draw upon.

of following this format is to provide you with an extensive and thorough framework for realizing your long-term projections.

The images of seasonal transformation provided here were designed to be used symbolically rather than literally. This means you can use this program even if you live in the southern hemisphere and your winter begins in June, or if your growing climate differs from the one used here. However, another way to make use of this program is to personalize it by adapting it to your own circumstances, and we encourage you to observe and appreciate the changes that take place throughout the year in your particular corner of the world.

WINTER DARKNESS AND DREAMING
EXPLORING YOUR DESIRES AND OPTIONS

Capricorn
Structuring

The winter solstice, the shortest day of the year, marks a turning point. It is on this date that the sun begins its return from its six month descent into darkness. On the same date, Capricorn, the determined goat, begins its rocky but surefooted climb.

Traditionally, humankind celebrates this time of greatest darkness by lighting up its dwellings with yule logs, Hanukkah candles, Christmas lights. And this is what you will do as you begin your cycle of manifestation. Bring light to the darkness by illuminating your own dreams, wishes and unconscious potentials.

This is a time of long nights, and the very first thing you must do is dream up your objective. Take time now for meditating, keeping a journal and recording your dreams.

This is the time of revealing to yourself what you truly desire, of discovering new objectives.

Visualization: Imagine yourself to be a gardener. This is the time of year when all physical labor is at a standstill. Now you begin to dream of next year's plot. Think of all the different varieties of flowers or vegetables you would like to grow. Picture anything that has ever appealed to you, from artichokes and bananas to yams and zinnias. Let your imagination plant whatever it likes. In your mind's eye, look out over your frozen, snow-covered plot and picture it blooming with the fruit of your desires.

Aquarius
Evaluating

With the onset of Aquarius, the Water Bearer, you will pour out your ideas. The alertness, intuition and inventiveness of Aquarius will serve you in evaluating your ideas. Give yourself the suggestion at bedtime that you will follow up the probabilities that branch out from the notions you've been forming. Note your daydreams and other conscious attempts to break out the many options you have provided for yourself. From the brainstorming of Capricorn, you have moved to the experimentation of Aquarius.

Visualization: Like every gardener, you look forward to the arrival of the new seed catalogs. Now you pore over pages filled with images of lush growth, looking up the varieties that interest you most. You study their qualities and compare them to the properties of your own garden. Which would thrive in your climate? How might the soil or the size of your garden be altered to accommodate new strains? It is the weighing of these variables that will lead to your decision about what to plant. You begin to sketch the layout of your garden, determining when you will plant each variety and where it will grow best.

Pisces
Deciding

The constellation of Pisces stretches out farther than any other, its two fish pointing away from each other, one toward Aquarius and the other toward Aries. Having experimented with various possibilities in Aquarius, you have arrived at the time of decision. In Aries, you will get down to the business of actualization. Now is the time of preparation.

In Pisces, the winter as well as the zodiac itself break down to dissolve into a new cycle. Now you must break down your objective into achievable smaller steps.

Visualization: You fill out and mail the order forms for the seeds you have decided to plant. The weather becomes less frigid and more rainy, washing away the winter and making the earth ready for new growth. On a cold but sunny morning, you don your waterproof boots and work gloves and go out to the garden to turn the soil. It is cold but no longer frozen. Working your spade to turn under the detritus of the winter, you feel the earth give itself over to your efforts as you aerate the soil.

SPRING PREPARATION AND PLANTING
BEGINNING TO CULTIVATE YOUR OBJECTIVES

Aries
Planting

The ram begins the zodiacal year as spring thrusts forth. In winter you explored options and finally chose a goal. Just as meditation and imagination were necessary in the beginning, now it is essential to perform a physical act. When you act in physical space, you anchor your projections in the earthly reality. In Aries, what you have been treating as a possibility becomes an intention in your thoughts and actions. This is the time of initiative.

Visualization: After breaking up the larger clumps of earth and crushing them in your hands to make fine soil, you make furrows in the garden to plant your seeds. After dropping each seed into the furrow, spacing each carefully and pressing it to its proper depth, you cover the furrow with the soil and pat it gently but firmly.

Taurus
Energizing

This practical, productive earth sign is the time for cultivation. This is the stage where the power enters the earth; you ground that power by doing physical things. Your acts in Aries are beginning to show forth, and you need to follow through so the next steps can take place.

Visualization: The first rows of green appear in the garden. You come to see and appreciate your young crop. How is it those small seeds knew how to become identifiable plants? You wonder over this simple miracle as you admire the tender new growth, and wonder at its variety: the reddish beet, the feathery carrot, the twining pea. The manifestation is underway.

Gemini
Exploring

The sign of the twins is intelligent and lighthearted, and this is the time for you to make observations, to be gregarious and scatter yourself. Your curiosity and interestedness increase your anchoring esoterically. You come to understand what responses you will get and why. The reason you are physical is to focus meaningfully, and now you can rely on a natural urge to spread out, learn and understand. This stage provides you with the information you require to bring your objective to full growth.

Visualization: The plants in your garden are developing quickly, you observe how each variety grows and spreads. You consider and decide which need to be staked, or thinned, or transplanted. As you gain understanding, you learn how best to weed, water and feed each one.

SUMMER GROWTH AND DEVELOPMENT
TENDING TO YOUR OBJECTIVE

Cancer
Nurturing

This sign begins as the sun reaches its apex in the yearly cycle, the longest day of the year. Because of the understanding you gained in Gemini, you are ready to really put your whole personality into your projection. The sun, the earth's source of energy, is now in full force. What was embryonic in the spring now flourishes in the extended light and warmth of summer. Cancer is the sign of nurturing, as you now nurture your thought forms.

Visualization: The plants in your garden are now stable and growing every day. You assist in their development by staking up vines, preventing weeds from interfering with their growth and cultivating the soil around them.

Leo
Maturing

This sign of the sun is the time when the earth's energy is hottest and highest. Open your projection to the intense light and heat. Bring your full personality to bear as you have now grown into an experienced maturity.

Visualization: Your garden is lush with growth. The fruits are swelling and ripening, and you care for your plants by keeping them well trimmed, weeded and watered.

Virgo
Harvesting

Your projection approaches fruition during this sign of the earth and its bounty. It has ripened with your attention and deliberate efforts to cultivate it. Now you loosen your grip on it a bit, for it is coming into its own by itself.

Visualization: Your vegetables are easy to pluck from their vines, for they have fully ripened. Weeding, cultivating and watering are less necessary now. You fill your baskets with your harvest, the product of your labor and ministrations.

AUTUMN HARVEST
REAPING WHAT YOU HAVE SOWN

Libra
Weighing

The equinox, the day of equal day and equal night, begins the sign of Libra, the scales. This is the period when you weigh what you have created through your manifestation. Consider what you have gained and lost, in preparation for the decision-making of Scorpio.

Visualization: This is the time of separating the wheat from the chaff and of preserving the best fruits of your labors. As the productivity of your garden slows, so do your activities, and you are able to use this time to reflect on your efforts and their results.

Scorpio
Eliminating

In the sign of Scorpio, the night begins to prevail. It is the time for moving indoors, of deciding what you will keep and what you will dispense with. Having weighed your manifestation in Libra, now you decide what you wish to keep or continue, and what you do not want or require. If you have been unsuccessful, this is the time when you pick yourself up and reorganize.

Visualization: As frost threatens, you make a last gathering trip to the garden. You discover and pick the last vegetables, leaving behind those that have failed to ripen or have rotted. You have prepared yourself for the winter with all that was good from your garden.

Sagittarius
Appreciating

The symbol of this sign is the archer, shooting toward the stars. Sagittarius is philosophical, logical, expansive. This is the time for looking over the whole and acquiring perspective. Enjoy and appreciate what you have brought about; this is the time of feasting and thanksgiving.

Visualization: The garden lies quiet and peaceful under the first snow of the year. You look out from your warm home, enjoying the rest you have earned from your labors in the field.

USING THE SEASONAL VISUALIZATION

In order to make this symbolic visualization more realistic, we are providing a fictionalized account of how one woman used the seasonal visualization in her own life. You may read it as an exercise, and apply the principles of each step to the events and activities in this story of Sally, a nurse with a husband and two children.

Structuring

in Capricorn

Upon reading Bernie Siegel's *Love, Medicine and Miracles*, Sally learns the importance of love and forgiveness, and wonders if she can use these principles to improve her relationships. After a dream where her father became one of her patients, Sally decides to begin with him. Sally's father is a difficult man whose drinking habit had made Sally's upbringing painful at times. Though he stopped drinking some years before, Sally knows that she still harbors resentment toward him.

Evaluating

in Aquarius

Discovering the relief in laying down her feelings of resentment and antagonism toward her father, Sally imagines the other relationships she might improve in the same way. Her husband, Ralph, is also prone to drink too much.

Might she change his habit by being more tolerant and forgiving toward him?

Deciding
in Pisces

After a weekend of heavy drinking, Ralph becomes particularly nasty and Sally spends a day and night in tears. Obviously, her strategy is not working. Confused and miserable, she decides to seek out counseling.

Planting
in Aries

Sally starts to see a psychotherapist. Discussing her relationships with both her father and her husband, Sally begins to understand how much alcohol has contributed to her unhappiness. She resolves to change that. She confronts her husband about how unhappy she feels about his drinking and extracts his promise to control it.

Energizing
in Taurus

Sally starts using meditative and visualization techniques to help improve her husband's habit. Becoming more and more determined, she closely monitors the amount he drinks. He reacts to her watchdog approach with resentment and anger. At her therapist's suggestion, Sally begins reading about the whole area of alcohol abuse.

Exploring
in Gemini

Sally learns from her research that she cannot control someone else's drinking and also discovers Alcoholics

Anonymous. She stops trying to influence Ralph's habits. Not long afterward, Ralph wakes up from a particularly wild night and announces that he's going to quit drinking altogether. He feels rotten, and asks Sally to throw out the rest of his vodka. She is happy to oblige him, and offers to drive him to the nearest AA meeting. She is delighted when he agrees to go.

Nurturing

in Cancer

After two weeks of success, Sally, who has been silently monitoring Ralph's attendance at AA meetings, is shocked when her husband "slips." Distraught, she locks him out of the house, then is filled with guilt and remorse. She decides to be more sympathetic and forgiving toward Ralph, but her therapist suggests that she work on herself.

Maturing

in Leo

Sally works on her own roots in an alcohol-abusing family. She "blows pictures," dissolving in her mind's eye the patterns that she learned growing up. In therapy, she works at differentiating between her husband's problems and her own problems. As Ralph's drinking returns to its former level, Sally begs him to return to AA.

Harvesting

in Virgo

Sally's desperation over Ralph's drinking increases until, during one tirade against her children, she recalls an ad for Al Anon: "You can see what it's doing to him. Can you see what it's doing to you?" She begins to attend Al Anon meetings and soon after, Ralph once again asks her to throw out his vodka. Sally declines, letting go of taking responsibility. Ralph discovers that he cannot throw out the liquor himself. He decides to go to marathon AA meetings over the course of a weekend, and manages to get back on the wagon.

Weighing
in Libra

Sally's children begin to attend Al Anon meetings with her, and her daughter writes a school paper on alcoholism. Ralph continues to attend AA meetings, and they begin to talk together about "the family disease." Sally's interest in recovery leads her to interview for a job at a drug and alcohol clinic.

Eliminating
in Scorpio

Sally and Ralph leave for their vacation, and on the way Ralph mentions having a drink when they arrive. Sally checks her impulse to burst into furious tears and instead tells Ralph in a neutral tone of voice, "If you have a drink, we are then on separate vacations. I'll see you if and when you get home." Upon their arrival, Ralph finds and attends an AA meeting. Sally meditates on detachment.

Appreciating
in Sagittarius

Sally starts her new job at the clinic and finds the work more satisfying and rewarding than her hospital job had been. At Thanksgiving dinner, she sees her parents and realizes how much has happened since her decision to forgive her father. Getting help for herself, learning how to deal with her husband and sharing with her children have opened up a whole new life for her.

It is fascinating to look back on your life after a year has gone by. You often will notice a coherent structure among the changes that arose quite spontaneously. Emergencies will come up, new ideas will occur to you, unforeseen alternatives will present themselves, and different themes will weave in and out of the year in ways that initially seem unrelated. But at the end of the year, you may see that this spontaneity has taken you on a tour around your self, so that you have seen yourself front, rear and side. The experiences of Sally illustrate the interweaving and spontaneity of growth.

WORKING WITH SEASONAL CYCLES

Because the visualizations and meditations here are long term, they may seem rather abstract. However, we want to impart the importance of getting to know the rhythm and cycle already embedded in this reality. There is nothing more practical.

One project that we urge you to undertake is to make it a point to step outside every couple of weeks and make observations of the rhythms of nature. Keep a simple notebook and jot down the weather, any animal life, the state of the vegetation, and the positions of the sun, moon or stars. See if you can sense the earth's inner light or sound, which changes along with the observable phenomena. This inner light or sound will probably lie just beyond your perception and leave you with only a sense that you have experienced something. Still, this impression of almost hearing or seeing is important and should also be recorded. Keep this up for a year or more, rereading your entries whenever the mood strikes you. This practice will help you to apply nature's archetypes to your own life and objectives.

14 Do-Be-Do-Be-Do Doing and Being

PEOPLE RIGHTLY ASK how life can be good if awful things happen. Coming to some peace with the fact that awful events happen is vital to the practical psychic. Even if your life proceeds along without disruption for years at a time, there is still pain in the world. As you become more competent, your scope of activity increases and you inevitably come into contact with events that don't turn out as you would wish. Even a Buddha, Christ or other enlightened being must deal with the fact that the people to whom he or she ministers do not all "get it."

Years ago, when John had learned just enough about psychic reality to mess his life up thoroughly, he asked a spirit one day at the Ouija board, "When does this all get to be fun?" He was expecting an answer such as, "when you learn perfect love," or, "when you get to the Buddhic plane," or some such cosmic answer. But the answer was, "as soon as you get a sense of humor."

It was a terrifying answer, because this was the first direct experience John had with the implications of the fact that you never stop growing, whether you're an ordinary person, an enlightened being, or a practical psychic. And if you never stop growing, then you never stop making mistakes and you never get to the point where you don't have to laugh at yourself.

In the beginning of the book, we compared learning to be a practical psychic to learning to be a jazz musician. For the latter, the steps are learning to play notes, then sounds, and then jazz. For you, the practical psychic, the separate techniques that you learned are the notes. Putting them together through time is the "sound." When you finally engage the fun and playfulness of life, you will hear the jazz.

That fun and playfulness come from two sources. The first is from an ever deeper perception that all life has meaning, including the so-called mistakes—even the most heinous. This is a point which can be discussed but never explained. As you become more psychic you will begin to see and experience directly the essential, ineffable validity of all life. It will come to you when you do not expect it.

The second source of playfulness is tied into the first. It is very close to the impulsiveness that was discussed in chapter 8. As you begin to recognize and identify with the intents of your eternally valid self, you will notice that your own true nature, your own true motivation, is focused on creativity and experience rather than "success." Conventional success becomes important more for the structure it gives the experience than for its own sake. It ceases to overshadow the joy of the experience itself.

Life then becomes a dance of doing and being, being and doing. A bit of grafitti encountered long ago in a college men's room summarizes the transformation from sounds to music perfectly:

To do is to be.—R. Descartes
To be is to do.—W. Leibniz
Do-Be-Do-Be-Do.—F. Sinatra

APPENDIX I

KNOWING SETH AND JANE: JOHN'S PERSONAL ACCOUNT

I HAD THE GOOD fortune to study with Jane Roberts and Seth in 1973 and 1974. It is hard now to express the thrill my friends and I felt then at the radical concepts Jane introduced, such as probable realities, simultaneous time and the fact that "you create your own reality according to your beliefs."[1] Prior to Jane, the best information widely distributed was the comprehensive but sanctimonious and deliberately unreadable work of Alice Bailey who channeled "The Tibetan." Bailey's books were dominated by what might be called the persimmon perspective. Life left a sour taste in her mouth. Mortal experience was a snare to be risen above. To be spiritual was to kill the ego and emotions. You were to turn your will over to the governance of supposedly superior beings.

When Jane's books came out with a beautifully articulate, simple English explanation of the way reality operates, we felt like turn-of-the-century women shedding whalebone corsets. Perhaps the most radical concept Jane/ Seth introduced was that each of our lives has meaning to be gained in ordinary human terms. Of course, there are overarching realities, populated by beings of seemingly infinite love and wisdom who are available for help; but we are responsible to live our own lives for our own purposes.

---

[1]The quotes in this article are the best paraphrases I can remember of dialogue that occurred fifteen years ago.

While there are aspects of reality too grand for our conscious minds to contain, nevertheless our conscious minds are meant to be our most practical and useful tools. Further, we are part of nature, fully entitled to our due, just as the animals and angels.

Jane's classes fully manifested that exuberant embrace of life. On Tuesday nights, twenty to forty of us would converge on Jane's living room in Elmira, New York. We were all ages and from all walks of life. Most of us lived within an hour of Elmira, but each week a carload or two of the "New York boys" would arrive from Manhattan, five hours away. They would drive right back after class, reaching the city near dawn. Their raucous good humor was an important element of the class's spontaneity and jollity.

Jane set the tone for the class. There was nothing formal about her. We all sat on couches, chairs or the floor and discussed what had happened during the week. Sooner or later, someone would make a statement that Seth felt was important, and in he would come. (This always reminded me of the duck on the old "Groucho Marx Show," which would suddenly drop into view when a contestant said the "magic word.") Jane's glasses would come off, and with a booming, "Now," Seth would launch his commentary.

Seth was awesome. I had studied at Harvard Law School and some of my professors had been brilliantly articulate, but I had never heard anyone to compare with Seth. A major part of Seth's message was that life is meant to be fun. In this case, the medium was the message, because Seth clearly enjoyed himself. His obvious enjoyment contributed to his powerful presence, punctuated by such masculine gestures that you forgot you were looking at a 90-pound woman. Seth used Jane's intelligence and eloquence, which she had developed over years as a writer and poet, to fashion thought with an elegant clarity. The overall effect was of such power and brilliance that we were all stunned one night when Seth returned only a minute after leaving to say he had forgotten something. "You forgot!" one of the New York boys shouted, waving his hand in an expression of disbelief. Laughter and pleasure filled the room as good-natured bantering continued between Seth and the class. When things quieted down, Seth said, "Yes, I do make mistakes."

This also was a radical departure from the spirituality of the time. Prior to Seth, great emphasis was placed on the so-called Masters, who were thought to teach only out of devotion to service, more like a penance than a pleasure. The Masters were thought to be essentially all the same in their perfection. But Seth pointed out that all information is colored by the consciousness of the being giving it. He explained that the eternal uniqueness of all consciousness is fundamental to the operation of the universe. If we would only listen to our own experience as intently as we listened to him, he said, we would learn more than he could teach us.

One of the most beautiful experiences I had in the class was one night when Seth urged us to understand that his teachings were not sacrosanct. "There are people who have never paid any attention to Seth or to beliefs, and who never worry about spiritual growth, but who, in their simple engagement of life, go out on their back porch and look up at the stars and know that they are a part of—a meaningful part of—this vast universe. They have experienced the meaning of life." As Seth described such experiences, his energy filled the room with utter clarity. I understood that our experience of the sacredness of life would be personal and simple. It would require no dogma, his or any other's.

Seth didn't require our respect. One of the best known Seth stories involved a woman whom I later lived with for a time. In her first class, Seth called her by the nickname, "Dolly."[2]

"Fuck you Seth," she yelled as she jumped to her feet, "no one calls me Dolly!"

Seth was unruffled and undeterred. "I only called you that because that is the name you use when you talk to yourself."

Later she told me, with amazement, that she had indeed been using that nickname when she talked to herself. She actually changed her mind after that conversation with Seth and asked everyone to call her Dolly. The point is that Seth was undeterred and lovingly amused at someone's saying, "Fuck you, Seth." His only response was to help Dolly get in touch with an inner self, one which was more intimate and less serious than the personality she identified with. Furthermore, it should be noted that Seth would have gladly called Dolly whatever she chose; for Seth always treated everyone with an elegant courtesy.

An illustration of that courtesy is my favorite Seth experience (especially since I am now a channel myself). It involved a running joke between Jane and Seth. He had often, over the years, commented on the special pleasures of human life, remarking on several occasions that he would enjoy sharing a glass of brandy with his listeners. Jane, however, hated brandy and put the nix on that. One night in class, a particularly dramatic class member announced to Seth that he had brought a surprise. With a flourish, he produced a bottle of brandy, and in an allusion to one of Seth's lives as an early and inconsequential pope, declared, "I KNOW that you'll like it, because it's CHRISTIAN BROTHERS!" We all laughed, including Seth. Then Seth grew quiet and tender. He thanked the student and went on to say, "This dear woman allows me to use her

---

[2]This nickname has been changed to protect the innocent.

body. I would never breach that trust by using it in ways she hasn't given me permission for." Seth's tone and energy expressed his fondness and love for Jane. Its emotional intensity came from its utter authenticity. That night, though it was always a theme, his boundless respect for our autonomy was plain.

My feelings about Jane herself are more complex and ambiguous than my feelings about Seth. My personal admiration for her is endless, and I feel fortunate to have studied with one of the most influential figures of the 20th century. But after all, Jane was human and so am I.

I was drawn to her teachings because of their intellectual clarity. I believed, as I think Jane herself did, that if you relied upon your intellect, you'd never go wrong. But I have changed my mind and my beliefs since then. Now I teach that it's your sense of humor that prevents you from going too far off course!

Jane's challenges have brought me much insight during my own psychic evolution. In retrospect, it seems to me that her powerful perception—that we each create our own reality according to our beliefs—caused her to forfeit a certain balance. She recoiled so intensively from all that she viewed as irrational, dogmatic and conventionalized, that she was unable to accommodate the peculiar logic of paradox.

For example, an understanding of the necessity for (and rightness of) individual autonomy was one of the gifts Jane gave to the world. Nobody else before her came close to understanding the enormous power and range of the conscious mind and the centrality and rightness of each individual's autonomous desires. But the logic of creating your own reality is organic and contradictory. Although it seems a paradox, autonomy cannot be sustained without a kind of surrender to the facts of dependence and mutual interdependence. Jane stood almost alone, not merely because her vision was clearer than that of others, but also because she never learned to nurture and cultivate flawed belief systems. While Jane relished others' uniqueness and gave space to their idiosyncracies, she reacted excessively to any concept that might be considered irrational.

It is deeply ironic that Jane, the greatest psychic of her age, never got help from other psychics. She seemed to me to reject all psychic belief systems as illusory and to reject the very concept of getting help. Everyone needs belief systems even though every belief system is ultimately illusory. Also everyone needs help. Getting help is one of the natural pleasures of an interdependent reality. To get help from others, you must be open to their belief systems, at least open to playing with their ideas. All belief systems must necessarily be limited and contradictory, for an idealized perfection is never attainable. The protection against the inherent limitations of any belief system—chakras, for example—lies not in refusing to use a limited belief system, but in having several belief systems. Then, you will be able to use the appropriate belief system at the appropriate time. Jane did not develop the ability to play flexibly with belief systems, her own or others'.

All that being said, it must quickly be added that it is ludicrous to view Jane's limitations as failures. Jane's strong, stubborn will was the tool she used to batter through universal incrustations of old and outworn beliefs. As such, she reminds me of a running back in football, who intentionally builds his body into a magnificent instrument of muscle that is marvelous for football but lacks flexibility for other aspects of life. If Jane struggled off this planet at her death like a football player who has had too many knee and shoulder operations, she left as the Hall of Famer who has revolutionized the game. The glory and brilliance of that revolution enhances us all.

APPENDIX II

ON CONSCIOUS BELIEFS

MATHEMATICIANS SPEND a lot of time proving equivalence. Often, a theorem or definition which sounds radically different from another is logically equivalent nonetheless. These equivalence proofs give mathematicians the means for understanding the very fabric of the mathematical realities they are studying. Many of the great mystical traditions state their assumptions and techniques in radically different forms. It is very helpful to study different frameworks to see how they accomplish the same practical goals as other, seemingly quite different systems.

One central emphasis of the Jane Roberts/Seth system is difficult for many people to understand. Seth constantly stressed that not only do we create our own reality according to our beliefs, we create it according to our *conscious* beliefs. If you understand what that principle is equivalent to, you will not only better understand the power and uses of Seth's vision, you will increase your understanding and effectiveness in using other seemingly dissimilar beliefs.

For thousands of years mystics have proclaimed, "As above, so below." This meant, among other things, that by your conscious actions you could trigger sympathetic reactions from the deep self. An analogy which can illustrate this point is provided by the hologram.

The remarkable three-dimensional picture called a hologram is produced when a laser beam is directed through a special photographic plate. But the hologram is even more remarkable than it first seems, for if the holographic plate is broken, each piece will produce the entire holo- gram. That is, if you have a hologram of your house and it is broken into several pieces, directing a laser through any of those pieces will still create the original three-dimen- sional image of the house. The only change you will get from breaking the plate into smaller pieces is that the im- age gets fuzzier. But no matter how many pieces the plate breaks into, each shard will contain the entire image of the house.

Long before the hologram became a commonplace metaphor for the mystical identity of each piece of reality with the whole of reality, Seth stated that if you could somehow destroy the entire universe, except for some tiny portion of it, say your big toe, you would still have the en- tire universe. In "no time," you would have the entire uni- verse back again.

Since each piece or portion of the universe "contains" the entire universe, studying any particular piece of the universe can give you all the information you need about the universe. So it is perfectly correct to say that you create your own reality according to your conscious beliefs, be- cause your beliefs contain energy and that is part of the universe. In the same way, it is correct to say that you cre- ate your own reality according to your karma, as some teachers would have it—or according to your big toe.

This is not to say, however, that Seth's dramatic pro- nouncement about our conscious beliefs was meaningless or trivial. Understanding that Seth could rationally have cast his philosophy in many different ways, such as be- liefs, or karma, or forgotten childhood experiences, allows one to appreciate the artistry and intent of what he did say. Prior to Seth, most teachings about how to make mystical transformations centered on pulling people out of ordi- nary experience. But Seth proclaimed that the human race had grown up, that many thousands of years had been spent developing the conscious mind and that now we humans were ready to interact mystically with nature and each other from the center of our own conscious minds and conscious experience. It's not that Seth's philosophy was the one true way, or that the terms he used were required to accurately describe reality. There is no one road to spiritual and personal advancement, not Seth's or any other's.

Seth's central message was that your individual life has meaning and that you co-create your reality as part of a divine universal play. You are in the center of your own universe. Thus there is a special importance to your conscious beliefs.

Even with an abstract understanding of the philosophical validity of creating one's own reality with one's conscious beliefs, the concept is still tough for many people to accept. Chapters 6 and 7 describe how beliefs can lead to situations that seem unrelated. What happens is that the implications of beliefs are often not understood. Even when you're faced with an unpleasant situation, you can't always recognize what beliefs led to it. Seth called such beliefs "invisible." Sometimes the implications of known beliefs are invisible as well. In the example in chapter 8 of the perpetually victimized Laurie, she knew that she thought the world was a dangerous place, and that she thought men were better equipped to deal with those dangers. If someone had asked her the question directly, "Do you believe the world is a dangerous place?" she would have been able to reflect on her beliefs and answer that question. She would not have needed to go to a psychoanalyst or a psychic or other expert. The information was always within her ordinary grasp. However, even if she understood that you create your own reality according to your beliefs, making the connection between her beliefs and their implications when mixed with other beliefs could be difficult.

Even where the connection is difficult, it can eventually be made consciously. It doesn't have to be made consciously, but it can be. For example, some of Laurie's forgotten childhood experiences may have contributed to her feeling that the world was a dangerous place. In the instance of a belief engendered by experiences from early childhood, or other lifetimes for that matter, the belief itself is distinguishable from the events that gave rise to it. The belief is always consciously accessible even if the events are forgotten.

Once the connection is made between the belief and its implications, and the belief is recognized to be limiting, what can be done? There are powerful psychic techniques to change beliefs—some of which are covered in this book—that don't even require knowledge of childhood events or past lives. This does not imply that such knowledge is useless; often the easiest way to change a belief is to get the past life information. But it is never *necessary* to get such information. All the necessary information is accessible to the conscious mind.

APPENDIX III

PROBABILITIES, SIMULTANEOUS TIME AND CHANGING YOUR PAST

PROBABILITIES AND simultaneous time were two of the most radical and challenging concepts introduced by Seth.[1] By understanding them, you can understand how to change the past—literally. Of course there are practical limits, but they are much wider than we are likely to believe.

The concept of multiple probabilities is often encountered in science fiction, but other probable realities actually exist. Everything that could happen, does—in some way at least. There are actual physical Earths where the strongest of other probabilities are actually played out. Whenever you strongly consider important issues, such as career, marriage and childbearing decisions, the primary options are actually played out. There are other planet Earths where other yous follow the paths you didn't choose in this life. To these other yous, this you is just a probability. To each of them, you and the others are merely a probability, a concept.

Many people have trouble with this idea of probabilities, wondering what their responsibility is for other probabilities and wondering if the fact that everything happens means that their choices don't matter. In fact, understand-

---

[1]This appendix constitutes an intellectual explanation. For a more playful and artistic exploration of these concepts, we recommend Jane Roberts *Oversoul Seven* novels. See the Recommended Reading section.

ing that probabilities do exist and that All That Is loves all experience does help you change your attitude about responsibility and the meaning of success. Following your impulses becomes more natural, and responsibility and success serve simply to help structure your reality, rather than to define its meaning (chapter 14).

For now, we want to focus on probabilities and simultaneous time to see how the past, and the future, can be changed. In our physical experience, one moment follows another and the past is gone forever. On a psychic energy level, this is no longer true. The energy from the past and future directly influence the energy of the present. Your energy in the present determines who you are now and what reality you create for yourself. If you have a painful memory from the past or an incomplete event in another life,[2] energy flows directly into your aura in this life. It helps structure your current beliefs. There are many ways to dissipate the limits from your past. You can work on your beliefs, and let your deep self make the change without your conscious knowledge; you can blow pictures of events that you either remember or psychicly perceive; and you can just live your life, working out your karma (uncompleted past events) as you go. One of the most powerful methods, however, is to change the past. This is possible because of the interplay of probabilities and simultaneous time.

Remember, to all your other probabilities, they are the real you and you are just a possible self. The same can be

---

[2]Incomplete events are ones that you haven't integrated into your soul. If you were tortured in another life and still harbor hatred toward your tormentors or retain the "victim" beliefs that led to the events in the first place, you will continue to have problems. You will have to de-energize the event by having your deep self make the changes, by blowing pictures, changing the past, gaining new experience, or some such manner.

said of your past selves. Let us say, by way of illustration, that in 1645 Joe was an English judge and ordered someone hanged. There are other probable selves of that judge who made different legal rulings, and even other probable selves who decided not to be a judge at all. So, if all of those probable English jurists are equally valid, whose energy and incomplete business affects Joe today? They are all real and valid. However on a psychic level, one of those probabilities will be the one that is Joe's true past—the others will only be probable pasts. The true past is not linked to Joe by some scientific law: it is linked to him by psychic energy. By definition, the true past is the one whose energy most strongly affects Joe's current energy.

Since Joe can use practical fantasizing to change psychic energy, he can change the connection from one lifetime to another. Figure 2 on page 132 shows different probable versions of Joe's 17th century incarnation and his present connection with one of them. In figure 2, the one true past is the one connected to Joe by his present psychic energy.

Figure 3 on page 134, shows what happens when Joe changes his psychic energy. The former "true" past still exists but it is no longer psychically connected to Joe and therefore is now merely a probable past. Because it is no longer connected to Joe, it no longer affects him. There is a new true past—the English gentleman who worked for the poor. His actions, not the judge's, are now connected to Joe's current energy.

Some important questions arise. What if my past involves someone else and they don't change? This can happen. Your past will be different from theirs. If the pasts involve actual physical acts that have physical effects today, the changes will usually have to be "stirred" into the present slowly, in ways that seem to make sense to participants.

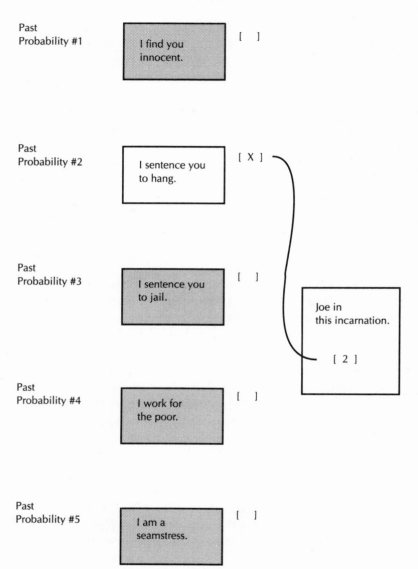

Figure 2. Lifetime in 1645. Here Joe's psychic energy connects him to probability #2. It is like an electric wire, and just as electric wires can be moved, Joe can move his psychic connection to a more desirable past.

Changing the past can have actual physical effects. Remember, now, you must be practical. Just as it is theoretically possible to walk on water, it is theoretically possible to change probabilities and all of a sudden be on the other side of the planet. But it is more likely that the *psychological* effects of the changed past will be experienced *first*. New beliefs will then be formed and new physical effects will take place naturally but unusually rapidly.

Changing pasts is an especially useful psychic healing technique. An AIDS patient, for example, could try a number of different approaches. If he knows when he was exposed, he could change the past in which the unprotected sexual encounter took place. In addition, he could investigate an array of creative changes, such as hooking up to a past in which the message of safe sex got to him earlier or one in which he became monogamous.[3] He might also relive some of his experiences where he let society's disapproval undermine his self-esteem, in order to accept himself and his sexuality at a deeper level. He could forgive those who have hurt him, hook up to his loving deep self, and begin lovingly to disengage from the chain of the past which led to his infection. Upon making these changes, he is still unlikely to wake up and find himself a new person who has never had AIDS, but he will find his physical and psychological health improving. He may or may not come all the way back, but his encounter with life will be deepened and made more pleasant.

Miracle cures can occur where probabilities have been changed. Due to the simultaneity of time, psychic alterations can cause change to occur very rapidly. When you change probabilities, you literally change the fabric sup-

---

[3]It is a simplification to say that you hook up to one true past. In fact you can hook up to several pasts, and when doing healing, try several. Accentuate the positive ones, and dissipate the negative ones.

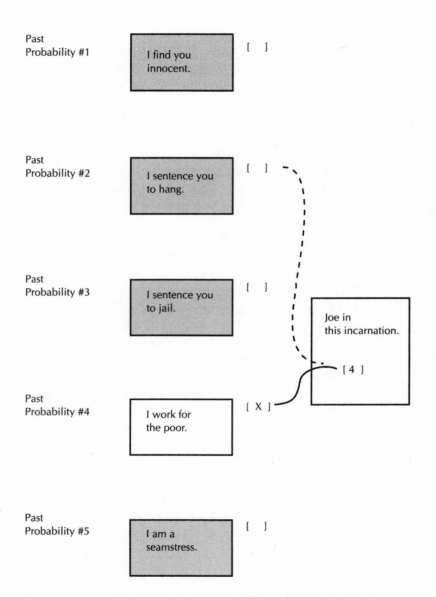

Figure 3. Here Joe takes the 1645 lifetime and adjusts the energy.

porting physical reality. Consequently, changing probabilities engenders enormous physical changes. Naturally,
those changes will occur in ways that are least disruptive
to our normal understanding of physical laws. Occasion-
ally there is no other way, and it will appear as a miracle.
But usually, the changes will appear as an unusually rapid,
or lucky, turn of events.

You can change your past quite easily. First you
"blow" the pictures of the old past by dissolving them into
a molten, golden sun (see chapter 7, page 37) and next you
fantasize the probable past you wish to hook up to as vividly as possible—seeing, feeling, and hearing the sensations in your body as intensely as possible.

You can use the techniques of changing your past for
big and small matters. If, for example, you have just had a
fight with a boss, spouse, friend or child, you can sit down
and work through your emotions and then change your
past. This exercise will not only greatly increase the skill
with which you handle similar situations in the future, it
will change the very energies around the past situation.
While the other person may still choose to hold on to his or
her resentment, you may be surprised to find that the entire event is more easily forgotten than usual, or that the
event is remembered more positively than you would have
expected.

RECOMMENDED READING FOR
THE PRACTICAL PSYCHIC

We have kept this list to a manageable length by including only those books we find to be especially useful because of their exercises or their special perspectives. Thus, we have both left out some favorites.

By, on, or influenced by Seth and Jane Roberts

Perl, Sheri. *Healing from the Inside Out.* New York: New American Library, 1988.

Roberts, Jane. *The Afterdeath Journal of an American Philosopher.* New York: Prentice Hall, 1978.

———. *Dreams, Evolution and Value Fulfillment, Vols. 1 & 2.* New York: Prentice Hall, 1986–88.

———. *The Education of Oversoul Seven.* New York: Prentice Hall, 1973.

———. *The Further Education of Oversoul Seven.* New York: Prentice Hall, 1979.

———. *The Individual and the Nature of Mass Events.* New York: Prentice Hall, 1981.

———. *The Nature of Personal Reality.* New York: Prentice Hall, 1974.

———. *The Nature of the Psyche: Its Human Expression.* New York: Prentice Hall, 1979.

———. *Oversoul Seven and the Museum of Time.* New York: Prentice Hall, 1987.

———. *Seth: Dreams and Projections of Consciousness.* Walpole, NH: Stillpoint Press, 1986.

_____. *The Seth Material.* New York: Prentice Hall, 1970.

_____. *Seth Speaks.* New York: Prentice Hall, 1972.

_____. *The "Unknown" Reality Vols. 1 & 2.* New York: Prentice Hall, 1977–79.

Stack, Rick. *Out-of-Body Adventures.* Chicago: Contemporary Books, 1988.

Watkins, Susan M. *Conversations with Seth, Vols. 1 & 2.* New York: Prentice Hall, 1980–81.

_____. *Dreaming Myself, Dreaming a Town.* Brooklyn: Kendall and Delisle Books, 1989; New York: Prentice-Hall, due 1992.

Books consistent with the Bostwick/Berkeley Psychic Institute Approach

Stevens, Petey. *Opening Up to Your Psychic Self.* Berkeley, CA: Nevertheless Press, 1984.

_____. *What's Your Psi Q?* Tiburon, CA: H. J. Kramer, 1989.

Wallace, Amy and Henkin, Bill. *The Psychic Healing Book.* Berkeley, CA: Wingbow Press, 1978.

Books that are channeled or about channeling

Hastings, Arthur. *With the Tongues of Men and Angels: A Study of Channeling.* Fort Worth, TX: Holt, Rinehart and Winston, 1991.

Moore, Mary-Margaret. *Bartholomew: I Come as a Brother.* Taos, NM: High Mesa Press, 1986.

_____. *From the Heart of a Gentle Brother.* Taos, NM: High Mesa Press, 1987.

Pursul, Jach. *Lazaris.* Beverly Hills, CA: Concept:Synergy Publishing, 1988.

Rodegast, Pat. *Emmanuel's Book.* Weston, CT: Friends' Press, 1985.

Roman, Sanaya and Packer, Duane. *Opening to Channel.* Tiburon, CA: H. J. Kramer, 1987.

Stevens, Jose and Warwick-Smith, Simon. *The Michael Handbook.* Sonoma, CA: Warwick Press, 1988.

Yarbro, Chelsea Quinn. *Messages from Michael.* New York: Berkley Books, 1979.

_____. *More Messages from Michael.* New York: Berkley Books, 1986.

Young, Meredith Lady. *Agartha.* Walpole, NH: Stillpoint, 1984.

Philosophy, physics and metaphysics

Berman, Morris. *The Reenchantment of the World.* New York: Bantam Books, 1984.

Bohm, David and Peat, F. David. *Science, Order and Creativity.* New York: Bantam Books, 1987.

Ferguson, Marilyn. *The Aquarian Conspiracy.* Los Angeles: Jeremy Tarcher, 1980.

Gyatso, Tenzin. *Kindness, Clarity and Insight.* Translated and edited by Jeffrey Hopkins, co-edited by Elizabeth Napper. Ithaca, NY: Snow Lion, 1984.

Kapleau, Philip. *The Three Pillars of Zen (Revised and Expanded).* New York: Doubleday, 1989.

Kline, Morris. *Mathematics: The Loss of Certainty.* New York: Oxford University Press, 1980.

Lao Tzu. *The Way of Life.* New York: New American Library, 1955.

Peat, F. David. *Synchronicity: The Bridge between Mind and Matter.* New York: Bantam Books, 1987.

Talbot, Michael. *Beyond the Quantum.* New York: Bantam Books, 1988.

Psychology—psyche and experience

Argüelles, José. *Surfers of the Zuvuya.* Santa Fe, NM: Bear & Co., 1988.

Bandler, Richard & Grinder, John. *Frogs into Princes.* Moab, UT: Real People Press, 1979.

Bandler, Richard. *Using your Brain—For a Change*. Moab, UT: Real People Press, 1985.

———. *Reframing*. Moab, UT: Real People Press, 1982.

Campbell, Joseph. *The Hero with a Thousand Faces*. Princeton, NJ: Princeton University Press, 1949.

Castaneda, Carlos. *The Fire from Within*. New York: Pocket Books, 1985.

———. *The Power of Silence*. New York: Pocket Books, 1988.

Faraday, Ann. *Dream Power*. New York: Berkley Books, 1973.

———. *The Dream Game*. New York: Harper & Row, 1974.

Jung, Carl. *Man and His Symbols*. New York: Doubleday, 1964.

LaBerge, Stephen. *Lucid Dreaming*. New York: Ballantine Books, 1985.

Monroe, Robert. *Far Journeys*. New York: Doubleday, 1985.

———. *Journeys Out of the Body*. New York: Doubleday, 1971.

Morris, Jill. *The Dream Workbook*. New York: Ballantine Books, 1985.

Ophiel. *The Art and Practice of Getting Material Things through Creative Visualization*. York Beach, ME: Samuel Weiser, 1967.

Palmer, Helen. *The Enneagram*. San Francisco: Harper & Row, 1988.

Regush, June V. *Dream Worlds*. New York: New American Library, 1977.

Reps, Paul. *Zen Flesh, Zen Bones*. New York: Doubleday, 1961.

Riso, Don Richard. *Understanding the Enneagram*. Boston: Houghton Mifflin, 1990.

Roman, Sanaya. *Living with Joy*. Tiburon, CA: H. J. Kramer, 1986.

Roman, Sanaya and Packer, Duane. *Becoming Your Higher Self*. Tiburon, CA: H. J. Kramer, 1989.

Sutphen, Dick. *Past Lives, Future Loves*. New York: Pocket Books, 1978.

Tart, Charles. *Waking Up*. Boston: Shambhala, 1987.
von Franz, Marie-Louise. *On Divination and Synchronicity*. Toronto: Inner City Books, 1981.
Wilhelm, Richard and Baynes, Cary. *The I Ching or Book of Changes*. Princeton, NJ: Princeton University Press, 1950.
Woolger, Jennifer & Roger. *The Goddess Within*. New York: Fawcett, 1989.
Woolger, Roger. *Other Lives, Other Selves*. New York: Bantam Books, 1988.

Body/mind connection

Borysenko, Joan. *Minding the Body, Mending the Mind*. New York: Bantam Books, 1988.
Brown, Barbara. *Supermind*. New York: Bantam Books, 1980.
Chopra, Deepak. *Quantum Healing*. New York: Bantam Books, 1989.
Hay, Louise. *You Can Heal Your Life*. Santa Monica, CA: Hay House, 1984.
Levine, Stephen. *Healing into Life and Death*. New York: Doubleday, 1987.
_____. *Meetings at the Edge*. New York: Doubleday, 1984.
_____. *Who Dies?* New York: Doubleday, 198e.
Rossman, Martin. *Healing Yourself*. New York: Pocket Books, 1987.
Siegel, Bernie. *Love, Medicine and Miracles*. New York: Harper & Row, 1986.
_____. *Peace, Love and Healing*. New York: Harper & Row, 1989.

General interest

Gawain, Shakti. *Creative Visualization*. New York: Bantam Books, 1982.

MacLaine, Shirley. *Dancing in the Light*. New York: Bantam
  Books, 1985.
_____. *It's All in the Playing*. New York: Bantam Books,
  1987.
_____. *Out on a Limb*. New York: Bantam Books, 1983.
Roman, Sanaya and Packer, Duane. *Creating Money*. Ti-
  buron, CA: H. J. Kramer, 1988.

Tapes and Sound Programs

Betar, Dimensional Sciences, Inc., P.O. Box 167, Lake-
  mont, GA 30552, 1-(800) 33BETAR.
Monroe Institute, Box 175, Faber, VA 22938.
Potentials Unlimited, Inc., 4808-H Broadmoore, S.E.,
  Grand Rapids, MI 49508.
Valley of the Sun, Box 3004, Agoura Hills, CA 91301.

Note to Readers

John is available for seminars and private psychic readings.
You may contact him c/o Samuel Weiser, Inc., Box 612,
York Beach, Maine 03910.

John is also working on a series of books which will
build on *The Practical Psychic*. Future subjects will include
sex and relationships, group and gestalt consciousness,
business and investing, justice and other topics.

Cynthia would like to hear from readers who have had
spontaneous psychic experiences, especially those that
concern family ties and other intimate relationships. Write
to her c/o Samuel Weiser, Inc., Box 612, York Beach, Maine
03910.

JOHN FRIEDLANDER'S metaphysical education began during his college days. In 1971 and 1973, he traveled and studied in India and Nepal. In 1973, he studied personally with Lewis Bostwick at the newly established Berkeley Psychic Institute in California. The next year, he went to New York state and joined Jane Roberts' Seth class. Keeping a low and lawyerly profile, John began to teach classes in psychic development in 1982. He formed the Practical Psychic Institute in 1988 and it has since become his full-time occupation.

John grew up in a small town in Georgia. He graduated from Duke University in 1970, and Harvard Law School in 1973; he passed the bar in 1974. For six years he worked in law firms specializing in business litigation, then opened his own general practice. John lived in Pittsburgh from 1977 until 1989; he and his wife currently reside in Ann Arbor, Michigan. John is pictured here with his cat, Hairy Professor Bodhicattva.

CYNTHIA PEARSON began her professional focus on metaphysical subjects with *I Ching: The Psychic Moment* (Cottage Software, 1985), which she designed and wrote. While working on a series of articles about channeling and trance states in 1987, she attended one of John Friedlander's lectures and they began collaborating on *The Practical Psychic* shortly thereafter.

Cynthia grew up in Pennsylvania, earning her English/Writing degree from the University of Pittsburgh in 1970. Besides designing software and writing, Cynthia teaches courses in psychic development and dream awareness. She resides in Pittsburgh with her husband, son and daughter.